ARE BOOKS DIFFERENT?

ARE
BOOKS
DIFFERENT?

Marketing in the Book Trade

Alison Baverstock

KOGAN
PAGE

BHTC

First published in 1993

Apart from any fair dealing for the purposes of research or private study, or criticism or review, as permitted under the Copyright, Designs and Patents Act, 1988, this publication may only be reproduced, stored or transmitted, in any form or by any means, with the prior permission in writing of the publishers, or in the case of reprographic reproduction in accordance with the terms of licences issued by the Copyright Licensing Agency. Enquiries concerning reproduction outside those terms should be sent to the publishers at the undermentioned address:

Kogan Page Limited
120 Pentonville Road
London N1 9JN

© Alison Baverstock 1993

British Library Cataloguing in Publication Data

A CIP record for this book is available from the British Library.

ISBN 0-7494-0900-2

Typeset by Books Unlimited (Nottm), Sutton-in-Ashfield, NG17 1AL
Printed and bound in Great Britain by
Biddles Ltd, Guildford and King's Lynn

Contents

Acknowledgements

I am afraid that since starting to write my first book, nearly four years ago, for most of my acquaintance, checking sections of manuscript seems to have become a feature of friendship!

Writing about your own profession is a very public pursuit, and I am enormously grateful to everyone who has read my material and made comments.

Most of all I would like to thank Dag Smith, whose idea it was that I should write this book, and who has supported me with continued interest throughout its development. I would also like to thank Jean Hindmarch and Orna O'Brien of Book House Training Centre; Philip Flamank of the Publishers Association; Paul Scherer of Transworld; David Teale of the Red House Book Club; Tim Farmiloe and Ian Jacobs of Macmillan; Andrew Welham and Liz James of Penguin; Simon Littlewood of Phaidon; Paul Richardson; John Jackman; Hamish MacGibbon; Desmond Clarke of ITPS; Richard Charkin of Reed Consumer Books; Matthew Huntley of Wells Bookshop, Winchester; Jane Hooper of Hoopers Bookshop, Harborne; Vivien James of Blueprint; Keith Howick; Jane Cholmeley of the Silver Moon Women's Bookshop; Jo Howard of Waterstones; John Cheshire of Heffers; Brenda Stones of OUP; Julian Rivers of Pentos; Bob Tyrrell and Richard Woods of the Henley Centre for Forecasting; Gina Allum of DataMonitor; Professor Michael J Baker of the University of Strathclyde; Dr Robert Grafton Small of the University of St Andrews; Dr Alex Gibson and Dr Simon James of the University of Exeter; Sally Butcher of KLP Promotions; Emma Blackley of Bounty Books; Alan Wherry of Bloomsbury; Brigid MacLeod; Joanna Mackle of Faber; Alan Roberts of HM Customs and Excise; Christina Thomas and Ailsa Macalister of the PPC; Sarah Mahaffy of Boxtree; Caroline Shaw of the Natural History Museum; David Rees; Cathy Douglas; Nicholas Jones; Wendy Tury and Ivor Powell of West Herts College; Professor Michael Twyman of the Department of Typography and Graphic Communication, the University of Reading; Clare Harrison and Leslie Henry of Book Marketing

Ltd; Robin Birn of Strategy, Research and Action Ltd; Lorraine Hinchcliffe and Nicola Potts of the Market Research Society; Philip Sturrock of Cassells; Jane Aspden and David Holmes of Dorling Kindersley; Kathryn Hislop; Olivia Hoskinson; Rosemary Roberts, Senior Lecturer in Publishing, Oxford Brookes University; Mr Croft of Threshers; Mr Shah of Bhags Pharmacy; Mr Singleton of M and J Hardware; Michael Cook of Balfours; Mike Hawker of Clothkits; Alan and Audrey Taylor of the British Independent Grocers' Association; Jo Wright of Tesco's Public Affairs Department; Cathy Boyle of the Leatherhead Food Research Association; Irena Springer; Colin Scott; Deborah Rea of Astron Appointments; Yvonne Messenger of the Independent Publishers Guild; Jack Daniels and Jean Gowans of the Careers Advisory Service, the University of St Andrews; Angela Mansell of Longman, Lindsey Fraser of Book Trust Scotland; Derek Searle; Hazel Hutchison; Sally Montague and Bill Jennings.

Finally, thanks to Neil for encouragement throughout, and to Jack for the deadline.

Foreword

AB's previous book *How To Market Books* successfully covered just about every aspect of one of the most varied and at times mysterious of all the disciplines in publishing. As a starting place, a handbook, it is still probably the best guide available for those already on this side of publishing and those who wish to enter.

Now she has expanded her potential audience well beyond those interested only in marketing. *Are Books Different?* has much to say about marketing but the canvas is broader, covering to a greater or lesser degree most of the key aspects of book publishing.

Needless to say, I don't agree with all the conclusions reached by the author, but then she wouldn't expect me to. Her prime purpose is to cover a great deal of ground, set out most of the relevant factors, views, pros and cons in all the areas covered, and arrive at what she hopes is a balanced view. Particularly interesting and thought provoking are the numerous quotes from those engaged in the industry now and in the past: by turns pithy, pretentious, provocative and puerille, they serve very well to illustrate what a curious collection of people publishers are, how ready we are to generalise from often narrow experience and how easily we strike exaggerated attitudes.

There are certainly too few books that give a good overview of the whole industry. This is an addition that will be very widely welcomed and used.

Introduction

It was said that the makers of *Butch Cassidy and the Sundance Kid* subsequently regretted killing off their heroes at the end of the film, as it ruled out a sequel. Did they momentarily toy with *Parents of Butch Cassidy* as *Butch Cassidy 2* was impossible?

The link between a block-busting film and this book may seem tenuous in the extreme, but the logic is there. On reading *How to Market Books* (Kogan Page, 1990), Dag Smith of Book House commented that, although he found it very useful, he felt that it got down to the nitty gritty of 'how' to market books before a thorough consideration of 'why?' had been given; there was lots of practical help but not enough theoretical advice. In short, an early chunk of the text was missing.

Where, he asked, were the chapters on what marketing really means, the principles it espouses, and some examination of whether the book trade adheres to, or departs from, them? Is the marketing of books really 'different', or is this just a rather refined excuse for failing to tackle book marketing either seriously or completely effectively. Is it possible to employ marketing fully in a product-driven industry? If it is, does publishing have to change? Can it change? What are the implications for the future of publishing? With the economy in recession and the book industry in particular in the midst of great change, it's a good time to think about these problems.

This book is the result. The first five chapters describe the problems and issues, and how they are being tackled at the moment. The remainder of the book discusses ways of dealing with them. It should ideally be read before *How to Market Books*, and I hope that those who find this book useful, or even enjoy it, will go on to do just that.

Alison Baverstock
March 1993

Chapter 1

Are Books Different? The Arguments For and Against

'Books are different' was one of the most tedious and sloppily thought out pillars of traditional publishing. It enabled many people, who should have known better, to ignore the new challenges of communications and of the leisure industry as the world changed in front of us. But there is a grain of truth in that shibboleth which persists, the clinical examination of which is, I suggest, an absolutely central and valid proposition for now and for the future.

(Michael Sissons, literary agent writing in the *Bookseller*, 12 April 1991)

So are books different? The origin of the phrase is the defence of the Net Book Agreement in 1962 and Arthur Bagnall's opening argument as to why books should be treated differently from other types of retail purchase.

The reactions I got when asking this question varied from finding the question 'rather embarrassing – it's such an old chestnut', to impassioned declamations about how they somehow have become so, but shouldn't be (how we got to this position produced yet more emotion). Several times there were puzzled smiles: how could I question anything so obvious?

Books are no different

It is perfectly possible to argue that books are no different. Publishing is a trade that seeks to sell its wares, like any other, and a book is a product with a price, just like a can of baked beans. The publishing industry produces a vast number of new and reissued products every year, but no one person or institution would be interested in buying them all, just as no single customer at Sainsbury's would buy every item in stock. It follows, therefore, that what publishers are doing is selling different product lines (or lists) to different market segments.

In any case, producing lots of different product lines is not completely unheard of in other industries. In the shoe trade, apparently every half size, in every width fitting, of every style, of both left and right shoes counts as a different product. The horticultural world changes fast too. Each year more than 5000 new plants are introduced into the UK, and there are apparently, already in existence world-wide, 25,000 different varieties of orchid and 463 of radish!

The fluidity of stock movement between bookseller and publisher, whereby what is on sale is effectively on loan, and what does not sell can be returned for a refund, is not unique. Paint is supplied to many retail outlets on this basis, and the stock for every promotion of a new food item in a supermarket is accepted on the basis of 'uplift' if the merchandise does not sell.

Announcing that you are employed by a fine wine company, work in television or do something 'in the City' (the 'what' never seems to be specified!) apparently has a cachet similar to saying that you work for a publishing house. Journalism is equally hard to get into, and determined aspirants often work in another capacity for the paper (say, secretarial or advertising sales) before getting into print. Advertising professionals compare the newly privatised utilities and financial service companies with publishers; both share a similar naivety about the methods of marketing.

And so on ...

Or are they different?

Yet die-hard book 'differentialists' remain unconvinced. Still the perception of a divide, whether stream or gulf, between publishers and the rest of the world persists. Are these differences industry-manufactured, and so all part of a huge conceit, or real? I thought the best way to start was by asking the opinion of as many people as possible, both within and without the book trade, and dividing the differences we came up with into two sorts: those that really do make the book industry different, and those that the industry has acquired, or encouraged, and now is disinclined to dispense with. In other words, the nature/nurture controversy as applied to the book trade.

Nature

1. The power of books as lasting vehicles for ideas
Books can change lives by making people think. The published product is

more than the sum total of its constituent parts. Indeed, perhaps the published product is not a product at all; rather, a packaging for the real product – the ideas or message contained within the covers.

The ability to publish provides first a voice and second a position in the 'establishment'. It is interesting to view Robert Maxwell's determination to acquire a national newspaper, and the general unwillingness of other newspapers and journalists to challenge such a public and litigious figure, in this context, or Rupert Murdoch's ownership of five British national newspapers and the international BSkyB without reference to the Monopolies and Mergers Commission.

And this voice brings with it further powers – or responsibilities. Students on publishing courses in Germany are taught that books are *Kulturtrager*, upholders of civilisation. Similarly:

> the printed word should be treated differently as it affects the whole question of free speech, debate and argument throughout the land
>
> (Michael Foot, 1962 debate)

> a book is more than its cover, pages and ink thereon. It is about ideas and values, and these have a price beyond its physical components.
>
> (Piet Snyman, *Bookseller*, 13 December 1991)

> books shape our imaginings and aspirations, and, through them, our reality ... publishers have a responsibility to question a book's moral impact on society and to reject those which could be damaging, however profitable.
>
> (Moyra Bremner, *Bookseller*, 6 September 1991)

Writing a book landed Salman Rushdie with a price tag of £2 million on his head. Are his publishers, and the reissuers of Sade, irresponsible, or are they brave in providing access to a variety of points of view? Similarly, the arguments about why you should not trade with hostile or morally dubious countries seem to apply in a different way when educational books, or titles spreading a different political ideology from that of the party in power, are the products in question.

> The role played by publishers in the human rights movement has been pivotal. This is because the basic work of protecting human rights begins with documentation.
>
> (Robert L Bernstein, chairman of Human Rights Watch)

Of course, this power to communicate does not apply to books alone – newspaper articles and television programmes can be far more immediate in their effectiveness. But while many other media of communication are necessarily ephemeral, because tomorrow's edition is being prepared as today's is seen, books smack of permanence. Why else have dictators tried to burn, or the politically correct to ban, them.

2. The role of the author and his or her copyright

A biochemist takes a job with a food company. He or she joins the laboratory working on new beverages and, along with colleagues, develops a new taste for a fizzy drink. It may go on to be a huge success, perhaps as popular as Coca-Cola $^{®}$, or a dismal failure, but the production details and the formula will continue to belong to the company for whom he or she was working when the product was first created. Should that person subsequently leave the company, the recipe will stay behind.

Publishers, on the other hand, have to deal with individual creators. Every manuscript they consider enjoys copyright owned by the author (unless the author is an employee and creates the work in the course of employment); the book has been written or prepared by that person, and he or she has enforceable rights over its future. Should the publisher sell the product for production in another format, to another manufacturer, in a deal completely separate from the original contract to publish, the original creator can still assert moral rights over the work by requiring to be identified as the author, and preventing derogatory treatment of the work, and this copyright can be continued by his or her successors until 50 years after the author's death. Looking further ahead, given that authors are the sole producers of specific items, publishers are perhaps moving closer to becoming licensed dealers or franchise holders.

Of course, moral rights can be judged to be of fairly minor importance, and if an author assigns copyright to a publisher, he or she can require identification and prevent derogatory treatment, but nothing else. Some countries ignore copyright completely, and piracy is common. Nevertheless, this involvement with individual creators is still a basic, and on a practical level significant, difference between the book trade and the rest of industry.

Nurture

1. The number of books produced each year

In 1992 nearly 79,000 new books and new editions were published in the UK. Even a smallish bookshop, if computerised, will probably have as many stock items on its records as a large supermarket. Yet there are relatively few strongly identifiable brands to divide up this output. Back in

1980 the *Lost Sales Survey* found that half the unsatisfied demand it identified was the result of books being unidentifiable by the trade; presumably the result of too many books in circulation, insufficiently differentiated.

There seems to be unanimity about the fact that there are too many books, so what can be done about it? Several publishing houses have made firm commitments to reduce their output.

Removing long-term uncommercial propositions from the lists will save money, as the reduction in costs from non-production will outweigh the loss of sales revenue (possible long-term successes must meanwhile continue to be subsidised). But in many companies basic expenses (for example, building rental, staff overheads, rep force) are based on *existing* sales levels, and as management will be reluctant to see those sales revenues drop, they may conclude that the margins on the other titles produced must be improved. This means that, for each title published, more of the print run must be sold and/or discounts to the trade must be lower.

Similarly, publishers trying to reduce the number of books they produce must ensure that those they do publish have more life in them: that publishers offer the best book, by the best possible author, or find an area of interest that is growing yet under-covered at the moment, rather than produce a 'me too' book on a subject area well served already.

Smaller houses, unable to pay the huge advances requested by agents on behalf of authors willing to change houses for more money, must take a long-term view of the authors they take on. They must spot nascent talent and nurture it in the hope of long-term literary recognition and financial rewards. And as mass markets are for mass producers, they must also become adept at spotting corners of demand that are too small or specialised for anyone else to bother with, and sell to them.

Alternatively, the basic cash flow lost through publishing fewer titles must be recouped through reducing overheads, making staff redundant and amalgamating their job functions, or awarding lower pay increases. If a firm is unwilling or unable to make cuts in any of these areas, an over-large publishing programme is often the inevitable consequence, and the cycle of too many books continues.

2. Each book is a different product

If there are too many books in existence, the situation is complicated by the fact that each title is an individual product requiring specialist and thoughtful market analysis and targeting:

> no two literary works are the same or alike in the way in which or the extent to which two oranges or two eggs may be said to be.
>
> (Justice Buckley, judgement in the 1962 NBA case)

Our problem is that you don't sell the product again to the public.
(Alan Wherry, interview in *Marketing Week*, 12 July 1991)

Publishers build lists in particular subject areas to make it more cost effective to approach that market (more titles equal more opportunities to sell). They try to create a reputation as a particular type of publisher in the hope of repeat purchases from a loyal market and of attracting authors who complement their style. But the fact remains that each published product is unique, and although customers have the power to recommend, most only buy a specific title once.

3. Books are cheap
The successful publisher's skill really comes into play here. Publishers produce vast numbers of books, each one requiring a slightly different market emphasis. Yet the price level at which they are sold, for the most part, precludes allocating the budgets required to probe those markets fully. We are selling a niche market product at mass market prices.

Publishers may talk about producing 'mass market paperbacks', but this is a relative term given that regular book buyers constitute only about a third of the population, and the initial print run for a mass market paperback title is usually around the 14,000 mark. (True mass market products are items such as Mars bars and videos.) Trying to promote its wares on over-stretched budgets has produced two contrasting views of the industry:

a)   publishers as speculators, creative people who can anticipate a trend on hunch, add belief to a good idea and go for it; make and lose money frequently, but on a relatively small scale.

A trade which seems destined to work within a climate of crisis.
(Sir Robert Lusty)

b)   publishers as inefficient and penny-pinching amateurs; publishing as a cottage industry in which financial profit is not the only aim of those employed – the stimulating atmosphere and 'fun' of the business are just as important.

4. The role of trade associations in publishing
The book trade is extensively monitored by professional bodies such as the Booksellers Association (BA) and the Publishers Association (PA), and a range of other formal and informal bodies.

These organisations are articulate, and frequently quoted in the media. Membership within the trade is substantial, despite the fact that major issues divide those who belong. For example, Dillons is opposed to the continuance of the Net Book Agreement and yet still belongs to the BA (without membership they couldn't have Book Tokens).

Many other industries have professional bodies, but more often these tend to cross over industrial sectors and link those with common job functions. For example, accountants, directors and buyers get together regardless of the particular market sector in which they work.

5. The nature of the published product

Publishers are conscious that they produce and market a product of the intellect, of the mind. Several people I spoke to referred to publishing as being 'different' from other industries because it produced something that was both good for people, yet not a life-essential such as dog food or toothpaste.

Kotler has advanced the theory of products having a 'care benefit': the contract between purchaser and retailer is based on an understanding of what you buy the product for, the object or service itself, but there are extra factors that augment the basic buying decision. Thus the same book can entertain, educate, supply status and show good taste, competing with different products in each of these markets.

In wider industry, most firms would seek to make a 15–20 per cent profit on net returns. In the book trade publishers are doing well if they achieve 5–10 per cent. Average wages in the book trade tend to be lower than in other industries, and many publishers are conscious, whether vaguely or explicitly, of their own professional altruism or, as someone with experience of the US publishing industry referred to it, 'social contribution'.

There are many difficulties for the firm promoting writing, not least that their product demands that the market is literate. Magazine publishers (whose buyers also frequently call the product they purchase 'a book') faced with similar problems have chosen outlets where their potential customers already feel at ease and sell accordingly. But publishers have been slow to do this; a large percentage of the population never go into a bookshop and feel uncomfortable doing so. Many people who might consider buying books as presents are dimly aware that some books are better than others, and consequently cautious about revealing a taste for ill-thought of authors.

6. Public and private attitudes to books

In trying to promote writing, publishers are alternately assisted and hampered by various forces from both government and society.

Government protection

There is no VAT on books and newspapers, unlike other forms of entertainment and instruction such as theatre tickets and museum entrance. This is to keep prices lower and make information affordable to the widest possible sector of the population, for the same reasons as there is no VAT on children's clothes or most items of food.

But the same legislation that exempts a child's fiction title and the quality dailies from VAT also exempts pornographic magazines and the tabloids. More reading material is bought on a Sunday than any other day of the week, but the restricted wholesaler-determined availability of newspapers (currently supplied to newsagents and some supermarkets only, and being investigated by the Monopolies and Mergers Commission) and government restrictions on Sunday trading mean that very little of it is sold through bookshops, and that almost none of the expenditure is on books.

Similarly, only net books and some pharmaceutical medicines have survived as the beneficiaries of government net price protection; they cannot be resold at less than the manufacturer-set retail price. In every other trade the manufacturer sets a recommended retail price, but the actual selling price is decided by the retail outlet. In other retail trades, offering branded goods at below the recommended retail price is a common gambit to get customers into shops, but attempts by manufacturers to *insist* that retailers do not sell beneath their recommended retail price are likely to be ruled against the public interest. (For example, in the spring of 1993, Kelloggs refused to supply any of their products to cooperative stores in the north of England, after a dispute over the low pricing of their cornflakes. The problem was referred to the Monopolies and Mergers Commission.)

It is surely ironic that the result of argument over these valuable practices is to draw attention to the price of books; to insist that the market for books is price-sensitive; that a finite value for books exists and must be defended. Meanwhile, the CD industry effectively ran a cartel and was allowed to get away with it by the Monopolies and Mergers Commission, which has claimed that the industry can charge what the public will pay.

Successive Secretaries of State for Education have emphasised the importance of children's education, yet their budgets place continual pressure on the prices that educational publishers are able to charge for what are, after all, commercially produced materials. Teachers, battered by continual pressure over what they want to spend, often seem to regard the economics of textbook production as immune from commercial reality. A tabloid newspaper with indifferent and sporadic colour – the cover price heavily subsidised by the revenue from advertisers – may cost 50 pence a day, but a full-cover, well-produced and bound 200-page textbook, with no pages lost to advertisers, is deemed expensive at £5.99.

Public attitudes

A view seems to have developed that free access to information is a basic right, and should not be paid for at all. Books 'are such a good thing that many people believe that, like air and water, they should be provided free'. (Trevor Glover, Penguin).

Parents in a Parents/Teachers Association will raise funds for school trips or a new swimming pool, but may resent the cash being spent on books (because they see their provision as the education authority's responsibility). Rattle the collecting tin for sponsorship from local businesses and if you ask for anything other than school books you will probably get a donation. Ask for money for books, and you get a lecture on government finances.

Similarly, no library could be expected to stock every item, but some public librarians set their ideal collection standard very high, claiming that charging the public for inter-library loans is iniquitous because it is wrong to make the reader 'pay for the inadequacies of the stock provided by the library' (*Bookseller*, 24 April 1992).

As well as being cheap (see point 3 above), books are also good value for money. The arguments are familiar: cinema admission costs at least £5.00; a round of drinks the same; a meal out considerably more. The *Books and the Consumer Survey* (see Chapter 6 for more information) was optimistic about public perception of books as providing such value for money.

But the nature of demand is that it is based on the consumer's perception of the product, and anyone who works in publishing must have had to defend the value of books many times, frustratingly often to people who can, and do, pay much more for other leisure pursuits, but somehow conclude that books alone are over-priced. Whatever the eventual outcome of the campaign against the Net Book Agreement (NBA), the end result is likely to be a confirmation in many people's minds that books are unnecessarily expensive.

Books provide a source of entertainment and information that, once bought, can be lasting, particularly in some publishing sectors. Consumers may give or throw away novels that they have read once, but reference and information books tend to stay on the shelves once purchased. This perception of permanence can work against the producer, as reference publishers have found when trying to persuade the general public that dictionary buying is more than a once-in-a-lifetime event.

Books also seem to be regarded as a slightly different kind of purchase by the general public. Is it because more involvement in the decision to spend is required? No other product requires such commitment from the purchaser, at such a low purchase price. In the same way, booksellers may be required to invest an enormous amount of advice and service in a small-scale purchase and, after benefiting from the information, display and cataloguing services of one bookseller, the punter may decide to buy elsewhere. Of course, the same is true in many other buying situations, but the retailer selling hi-fi or expensive clothing makes more on each actual sale to cover the costs of the enquirers.

7. The desirability of market research

One central tenet of marketing to most manufacturers is the need for formal market research:

> Market research drives the marketing process as it provides the facts which stimulate the innovative process and ensures that the company grows in relation to consumer needs.
>
> (Robin Birn, market research professional)

Yet this is an area on which publishers, as a general rule, spend little time and money, and so have relatively little experience. What is spent is frequently absorbed in-house under general overheads, as it is often carried out by new recruits or by those engaged in other related jobs. Book Marketing Ltd (BML), which offers industry analysis and tailor-made research services to the publishing industry, carried out by industry specialists, and at competitive rates, is finding that much time is spent by their staff helping the book trade to interpret the data.

It is almost certainly easier for academic and educational firms to locate and quantify their markets – the number of academics teaching a particular subject or the number of secondary schools does not change very much. They can then make enquiries of sectors of the market, and usually this is done by in-house staff.

Among general trade publishers, whose markets tend to be more amorphous, those firms which do spend on market research are frequently those with a strong brand image such as Mills and Boon or Reader's Digest. The more literary houses may dismiss them as over-reliant on specific markets, but such firms also inspire envy in their competitors, who admire their success and wonder how to get into their markets without the initial investment.

The book trade's views on the necessity of market research are the result of a combination of the 'different' factors already discussed: shortage of money; a vast number of new titles coming through to be considered;

familiarity with, and confidence in, judging a new project on past experience. Many publishers argue that, given the creative nature of the industry, market research would be unable to predict bestsellers as effectively as experienced hunch ('we already employ brains, what is the point of paying for other people's?'). And that if you only produce what people have said they want, you are not anticipating trends and hence shrinking the potential size of your market. For example, it is unlikely that Stephen Hawking's *A Brief History of Time* would have shown up well in market research, yet it has sold in huge quantities. But, on the other hand, as Trevor Glover told a BML presentation in early 1993: 'If we judge only by our own attitudes, we will be self-deluding and unrepresentative.'

Publishers who do commission market research usually take a long-term view of the likely payback, and many feel that publishing is too unstable at the moment to permit such a view. One marketing director speculated that many publishing houses are editorially led (although not always editorially run) and that editors are often sceptical of the value of market research. This is understandable in a time of job insecurity, but while market research may indicate the nature of demand, and hence lessen the risk of investment, there is still a need for executive judgement on what will satisfy that demand.

Market researchers may confess themselves amazed that an industry the size of publishing does not commission more from them, but then 'they would, wouldn't they', and of course the industry's collective size is fragmented between many different firms. Generic (as well as title specific) market research is taking place through Book Marketing Ltd (BML); generic advertising is not considered successful (see Chapter 4).

8. Distribution arrangements

The relationship between producer and retailer in publishing
Although the recent arrival of several new bookselling chains has shifted the traditional balance of power in the book trade, and it would arguably shift still further should the NBA go, the market for books is driven by the producer rather than the retailer.

The reason for this is that publishers effectively have a monopoly of supply, and this has a fundamental effect on the nature of the relationship between supplier and distributor. There is only one source for the new Jeffrey Archer or Dick Francis, however much rival publishers may try to argue that one author is as good as the other. Publishers have of late tried to get round this by creating writers out of names which are already well known, providing a ghost writer if they cannot write themselves. (The novels about racing by John Francome were a good example of this; he had clearly been positioned to become the 'next Dick Francis'.)

It is probably true that the more creative the product, the more likely it is to be product rather than outlet driven, and the position of books may be compared with designer dresses, fine art, indeed any product where the name of the creator is more significant to the buyer than where he or she buys it, hence a quality publishing house being able to boast (and they did) 'we are not market led'. Companies in other industries do survive without effective marketing, but generally not as well or as often as demand-sensitive suppliers.

Compare this with the position of a major retailer which wants to offer a new skirt for the coming season. After a design has been commissioned, and specifications drawn up, the job is put out to tender from a variety of suitable manufacturers. One will be awarded the contract and will be required to deliver according to the terms of that contract. In other words, production and distribution are retail-led, by retailers who use their huge customer base for continuous market research.

Responsibility in publishing

Publishers are distanced from their buyers, as they sell their wares, in the main, through retail outlets. Nothing new here, so do clothes manufacturers and vineyard owners. What is different about publishers is that, apart from a few firm sale commitments, they effectively rent their wares to shops, which can return what does not sell through sale or return. Many publishers I have spoken to feel this cuts out an important level of commitment from the book trade.

Part of what bookshops add to the actual volumes sold is expertise, largely based on customer awareness. It should be in the bookshop's long-term interests to learn their customers' needs, just as Marks & Spencer does, and order accordingly. But few promotional initiatives are trade led. The BA produces a Christmas catalogue each year but other initiatives have largely been one-offs, cancelled because of lack of support, or led by working committees of publishers. At the same time, publishers have seen a huge increase in the cost of promoting through bookshops – it can cost £3000–£4000 for a window display in a major chain store, even more to appear in their Christmas catalogues. Yet the involvement from retail staff in promotional ideas that are set up is often disappointing.

The sensitive nature of timing in publishing

All industries trying to sell their wares have to coordinate market life cycle and product life cycle; success comes from harnessing the two.

But the shelf life of books is complicated, and slightly different from other industries. To start with, there are the difficulties of a market structured on a 'two-bite' principle (hardback and paperback), neither of which will necessarily work on its own. Both stand-alone hardback and paperback houses have failed. Publishers also face the difficulty of trying to reach several different markets with the same sales and distribution organisation at the same time.

Then there is the relative importance of the 'new' product in the book trade. Sales levels at publication are crucial; books have a short time in which to 'make it' and if month of launch sales are not good, the title may never recover. In the same way, the two-to-four month point after launch for a mass market book, when titles are either reordered or forgotten, is similarly an important time.

And yet, in comparison with other industries, the backlist occupies a crucial place in the book trade. Obviously, statistics vary according to the kind of books being published, but one general house claimed that each year 75 – 80 per cent of the turnover generated in bookshops is from titles published more than a year ago (for children's publishers the percentage is even higher) and bookshops confirm this reliance on the backlist. In the grocery trade and the CD and tape industry, the emphasis on what is new is much stronger, and other retailers, such as clothes shops, have no backlist at all.

> The top 75 singles sales represent about three-quarters of the total singles market in any one week, and the top 75 albums about 40 per cent of the albums market. I am not sure how far this mirrors the book trade, but I'd imagine that your top 75 titles represent a much smaller proportion of the total market each week.
> (Adrian Wistreich, Chief Executive of Chart Information Network, *Bookseller*, 15 May 1992)

This reliance on knowing what is new and selling fastest has meant that recording companies collectively fund their own electronically maintained bestseller list, used in retail outlets as a marketing tool. Up to now there has been a variety of different bestseller lists maintained in the publishing industry – by Peter Harland of Bookwatch and by WH Smith, as well as other local initiatives. An industry-wide, computer-based and jointly funded list for the trade is currently under consideration.

9. The inward-looking nature of publishing

Publishing is an industry that often seems to look within for inspiration, rather than to the wider world outside: 'elitist, complacent, unprofessional and out of date' was how Nick Wells, Marketing Director for Reference and Dictionaries at HarperCollins, described it at the BML Conference in February 1993. There are several factors involved here:

- Publishing as a medium of communication, ideas, and above all civilisation, has sustained all involved in the book trade with a rather elevated view of themselves. A long-term snobbism persists about what many are unhappy calling an industry; publishing is seen as a profession rather than a trade, with, Wells contended, 'a lingering contempt for the marketplace where books have to be sold'. For example, when the professional parameters of competence for the National Vocational Qualification (NVQ) were being established, publishers protested at their initial classification under 'manufacturing'. They were subsequently recategorised under 'communications and media' and have so far maintained a singular resistance to the inclusion of exams in the various qualifications on offer, in contrast with almost every other sector of employment.

- There are still many privately run companies (there are nearly 300 members of the Independent Publishers Guild), and such publishing houses do not need to justify their existence to shareholders by making large profits. Even the larger corporations often report low percentage returns on capital employed. So does the value of the published product, as 'a vital long-term necessity to civilised man' (Arthur Bagnall, 1962) mean that low sales are seen as a victory for altruism rather than a disappointment?

- The demand for jobs in publishing always outstrips supply. The PA recently advertised a part-administrative, part-secretarial, job for a graduate with two years' experience of publishing. They got 650 replies, of whom over half had the right experience.

- Publishers are often accused of being happier in the act of publishing than marketing what they produce to the wider world:

  We are left with the abiding impression that publishers enjoy publishing, whilst actually selling the stuff obviously does not give them the same kick.

  (Jo Craig, Aloe Book Agency Pty, letter to the *Bookseller*, 28 August 1992)

Many concentrate on selling more titles to the same market rather than expanding the overall market for books. The ABs buy most books, but they make up only around 18 per cent of the population. Each year, Book Tokens Ltd concentrate their promotional campaigns on reaching those who buy for children, ignoring wider markets of those who might be.

interested. One publisher speculated that we are all publishing to impress each other.

– Publishers often worry about the wrong things; this is reflected in our 'industry speak'. Twelve years ago I remember Carmen Callil giving a talk to the Society of Young Publishers about starting her own business. She said she had always wanted Virago to publish 'trade paperbacks'. I didn't know what a trade paperback was, but I knew I found her dark green covers with painted portraits on the front, very collectable. Today it is still true that too many publishers become bogged down in formats rather than markets, hence the title of Andrew Welham's excellent paper to BML's 1992 *Books and the Consumer* presentation: 'Customers matter, formats don't.'

– Similar inward-looking trends can be seen in recruiting staff. Let's look at staff movement.

From publishing to wider industry

Publishers frequently job-hop, but seldom industry-hop ('the people are nice'; 'I love the variety'; 'I like working with books'). But do publishers fail to transfer because they prefer not to, ie because of an inertia factor, or because they are considered unqualified by the rest of industry? Is it true, as someone assured me, that marketing in publishing is still considered a second-class activity? Among senior management, transfers in from outside are becoming more common, but they attract a certain amount of snobbism. Peter Davis, Chief Executive of Reed, made his name in the supermarket world launching Angel Delight and later worked for Sainsbury's. But, I was told with great emphasis, 'no one would claim he is a publisher'. Surely his origins give him such a valuable objectivity on the industry he now works in:

> My observation of the book business is that it's very introspective and that people are very concerned about what they do as publishers or agents or booksellers or authors and not always enough about the person reading the book.
>
> (*Bookseller*, 24 January 1992)

From wider industry to publishing

According to Astron Appointments, the recruitment agency specialising in the book trade, most publishing recruiters look either for existing publishers with identical experience to their own, or for related publishing experience. Few want to advertise outside the industry, and only about 20 per cent of their vacancies are put into the *Guardian* as well as the *Bookseller*.

The reason for this is that any appointment is a risk, and appointing from a known background minimises that risk.

Those who leave the industry, say, for more money or to work on a different type of product, will often find it hard to get back into the profession later on. The reason for this is that the ex-publisher will nearly always find him or herself standing beside a 'pure' publisher, whose motivation is easier for the interviewer to understand. There is something rather threatening about those with external experience: will they find the home team terribly inefficient?

Lower down the job scale, education to degree level is preferred, and many publishers train their own recruits from scratch, say, through a secretarial start. For the able recruit, well sited in a company, this can result in a swift rise: Joanna Mackle at Faber rose from publicity secretary to publicity and marketing director in five years.

From dedicated publishing training courses into publishing

Nor do publishers in general make extensive use of the output from the publishing courses that are now available (for more on this see Chapter 8). There are now several colleges running courses in publishing, and each year around 200 students emerge on to the job market. Over half proceed, by choice, into a job outside publishing, and until Book House Training Centre gathered employers and course managers together recently, there were no formal links between the two. The only time Astron were told that a student from the Oxford Brooks University publishing course would be particularly favourably viewed was when the recruiting manager had himself been a student there.

Once within a publishing company, most training is 'on the job' rather than on courses. There is no UK equivalent of the North American course for senior publishers at Calgary University. There are few publishers who spend money on training middle management for higher things, in the way that BP will put high flyers through INSEAD or Cranfield, or the Armed Forces send people to staff college (although the number of people studying part time/in their own time for such qualifications is growing). Is this because we cannot afford to – tight staffing levels meaning that staff cannot be spared to attend – or because we are sure that, as books are different, we have nothing to learn? There are few publishers who arrive in the industry equipped with an MBA. (Philip Sturrock of Cassell did, but as his was acquired after university rather than after a period of industry and, as he went straight into publishing, his salary expectations were arguably lower.) Astron have never been asked specifically for an MBA; most publishers assume that they can't afford one; or that it isn't all that important anyway.

The conceit continues that every publishing house does things differently and it is consequently better to train your own staff than have to retrain. But if publishers do not accept the validity of cross-industry practice, it is interesting that publishers wishing to gain an NVQ in marketing must join the wider grouping of the marketing profession as a whole; the qualification is not just specific to publishing.

Conclusion

The nature of books as a different kind of product took about a page to describe, whereas the nurture of industrial practice took nearly ten times as much space. Perhaps we should conclude from this that books are a bit different, that publishers have become so, and that the major reason for this is the way in which the book trade has grown used to operating, rather than the public's perception of what books are for. Whether this position is tenable in the future is the subject of the remainder of this book.

Chapter 2

What is Marketing?

Whether books are definitely, slightly or no different at all from other kinds of product, there is probably general agreement that they have often not, in the past, been marketed as professionally, or perhaps as expensively. The argument about whether or not it is *possible* to market books in the same way as anything else is most logically begun by deciding on what marketing actually is.

This is not easy. And to those in the book trade, most of whom have no formal marketing education, it may make stodgy reading. But I do believe that some consideration of what marketing *is* provides vital background information to the subject of this book. 'Marketing' is a relatively recent term. The first widely quoted academic statement on marketing was provided by Theodore Levitt's paper on marketing myopia in 1960, and since then there has been unanimity only on the fact that it is difficult to agree on a definition. My publishers told me that the market for books in this area is already overcrowded, so it is probably presumptuous to try. Nevertheless, here goes.

I will start with a generally accepted use of the term 'marketing', and then proceed with more scholarly theory.

In everyday speech the term 'marketing' is used to mean 'sales related'. The British are frightened of the salesman or woman, and in this sense 'marketing' developed as a term to disguise the dreaded 'sales' word (for example, 'marketing executive' has replaced 'sales representative', 'tele-selling' is more commonly called 'tele-marketing'). The word 'marketing' has now itself become tainted with the same spirit. Someone standing in the street with a clipboard, claiming to be carrying out a market survey is, we have become convinced, most likely to be trying to trick us into buying life insurance.

A development of this view of marketing is an understanding of it as a process that can be *applied* to a business. In the same way as a firm may appoint a distribution director, they may decide to appoint a marketing director. But just as firms may decide to save overheads and not increase the size of the staff, those engaged in the business of touting for custom may claim that they do not believe in marketing as an effective means of doing this. They may decide that what are seen as typical 'marketing products', such as commissioning an elaborate letterhead, or creating a brochure they will not know what to do with once it is printed, are expenses they can do without. Point out that by pursuing customers they are already 'marketing', and they are surprised.

While these popular conceptions contain grains of truth, if you look instead to the growing body of marketing literature for a definition, a different emphasis starts to emerge. Of key significance here is the *concept of the customer*, and his or her importance to marketing.

> Marketing is the performance of a business's activities that directs the flow of goods and services from producer to *consumer or user.*
>
> (American Marketing Association)

> There is only one valid definition of business purpose: to create a *customer.*
>
> (Peter Drucker, *Management: Tasks, Responsibilities, Practices*)

> Marketing is the whole business seen from the point of view of its final result, that is from the *customer's* point of view.
>
> (Peter Drucker)

> Marketing consists of a set of principles for choosing target markets, measuring their needs, developing want-satisfying products and services, and delivering them at a value to the *customer* and at a profit to the company.
>
> (Philip Kotler, *Principles of Marketing*)

> Marketing is the commercial discipline which businesses have developed while trying to identify and respond to the needs and demands of consumers or other *customers.*
>
> (Chartered Institute of Marketing)

> Marketing is the creative process of satisfying *customer* needs profitably.

So, the key word seems to be *customer*, and our definition should probably centre on this complicated coordination of different factors with the customer at the centre. The customers' definitions of need and adequacy determine the nature of demand, for, in marketing terms, demand is only effective if customers have the need, the means and the will to purchase. The crux of marketing is that customers assess their own needs, in terms of their own circumstances, and select products accordingly; their values are what matter. 'No customers, no business.'

Turning back briefly to the popular conception of the subject dealt with above, marketing is thus the practice of putting the customer in the centre of the business. First, it means running, and if necessary changing, the business to meet the needs of the consumer – ironically the very person who often feels most alienated by the word. Second, marketing emerges as far more than the responsibility of a single department within a company. Properly managed, it should be a complex coordination of different but related factors, which effectively constitute the company, its operations and future. As Colin McIver put it:

> Marketing is not a self-contained discipline that produces results in isolation from other managerial functions, such as production, purchasing, personnel and finance. It's a vital management function that needs to be skilfully blended with all the other functions that add up to a successful business.

> (*The Marketing Mirage: How to Make It a Reality*, Mandarin 1990)

Marketing is thus:

- a *concept* (based on the primacy of the customer's needs);
- a *function* (the integration of different parts of the company to anticipate what the customer wants, and provide it);
- a *series of techniques* to that end (market research, promotion, advertising etc).

A company with a *marketing orientation* will put the needs of its customers first, and think about what it can make to meet them, as opposed to a *production orientated* company, which takes as its starting point 'what can we make?' and then thinks about who it can be sold to.

Marketing orientation
customer needs
↓
marketing plan
↓
manufacture product

Product orientation
Production capability
↓
marketing activity
↓
customer

Mastery of marketing is certainly not something that is instantly achievable. Good marketing must encompass long-term strategy and planning; keeping abreast of social, political and economic trends so that management can understand which way the market is moving; perhaps even lead it. This information and feedback should be used to refine the product range over the longer term: to prepare different versions of the product for different markets; to identify or perhaps create new market trends; to draft contingency plans; to react speedily to changed market conditions or new information. In short, marketing works best if it is adopted as a long-term philosophy for the whole company.

Checklists for achieving good marketing

Many different areas need to be considered, taking into account all product and market considerations, namely:

- company objectives; long and short term;
- market research; what needs/opportunities are there?
- estimating demand – actual, potential, latent;
- competition research;
- product research and development;
- product design and styling;
- production sourcing and standards;
- pricing;
- range and variety;
- inner and outer packaging;
- quality control;
- sales forecasting;
- promotional planning: advertising and merchandising;
- selling;
- budgeting: cash flow, investment and profitability;
- customer service;
- distribution;
- after-sales service;
- evaluation;
- development of more products to sell to the same market.

It is the coordination, or synergy, of these factors that constitutes effective marketing.

Various marketing people have tried to condense these considerations into snappy acronyms or more memorable lists. For example, in the 1950s the Harvard Business School came up with the concept of the marketing mix to deliver good marketing practice. This consisted of getting:

- the right product to
- the right people (the designated market) by saying
- the right things in the promotional message and choosing
- the right way (the creative strategy) at
- the right time and in
- the right place (sales vehicle or location).

The four Ps

These were first advocated by McCarthy in 1954, who recommended that good marketing should pay attention to the following:

- product;
- price;
- place;
- promotion.

And for the marketing of a service, the following should also be considered:

- personnel;
- process;
- physical evidence.

These mnemonics all work, perhaps best in combination, adding people (or designated market) and timing to the four Ps and price to the 'marketing mix', and also reordering them in line with the importance of the customer to marketing. Finally, profit should be added to both. Thus we have a combined checklist:

- people;
- product;
- price;
- promotion;
- place;
- (period of) time;
- profit.

It is worth looking at each of these elements in greater detail.

People

This is the market whose needs are met by the product, and are thus most likely to buy/or have it bought for them, followed by the wider distribution of potential buyers who might also be interested. Extensive market research before any decisions are made may help to reveal who they are and their needs (see Chapter 6 on market research).

Product

Marketing should consider:

- specifications;
- product benefits (basic, tangible and augmented);
- styling;
- functions;
- materials;
- inner packaging;
- range and variety.

This should be in relation to what else is on the market – direct and indirect competition. Some products are 'me too' items (soap powder and 'lookalike' blockbuster novels); some are substitutes (a gas cylinder heated brush instead of plug-in heated rollers; a new diet and exercise regime book that demonstrates how you can get slim by eating chocolate and skipping); others are completely new ways of dealing with existing or developing consumer requirements (the disposable nappy instead of the cloth variety; the first theory of evolution published for the general reader).

Price

Here again, there are many considerations:

- the financial needs of the company (to generate immediate revenue; to secure market leadership quickly or product quality leadership over the longer term);
- how large the demand is;
- the perceived value of the product;
- production/quantity equations. What is the most cost-effective number to produce? (Some raw materials are sold in specific unit quantities and ordering slightly less or more will disproportionately increase your production costs.) Will producing too many product varieties make the standard unit price too expensive?
- what is the competition doing? What are they charging?
- is it more cost effective to produce another 1000 while the production lines are running?
- the balance between price volume (the volume sold at a particular price) and profit. A calculation of the break-even shows how many you have

to sell to recoup your costs, and thus helps you to estimate the level of risk.

There are various means of calculating price depending on the above. Probably the most common is cost plus x percentage. The production costs are established, an allowance for overheads is added, and then the company's profit margin is added to produce the purchase price. This is reliable and a useful company standard, but it largely ignores market factors. Other methods of price calculation include: break-even analysis; target profit pricing; perceived value pricing; tender pricing and going rate pricing.

Once the decision has been made on how to calculate, the price needs to be expressed in the best possible way to make sure:

a) that everyone understands it (for example, what does £15.00 non net mean to a newly qualified teacher?); and that

b) it is as appealing as possible (for example, £14.99 sounds cheaper than £15.00).

The final thing to think about are the variants to list price:

- legal constraints on pricing, if any;
- special offers (pre-and post-launch prices);
- discounts/credit allowances offered. Discount levels for sales intermediaries will largely depend on how many other agents are involved; each one will need to make a profit;
- rewards for joint promotional activity, ie sharing risk and cost;
- a sliding scale of incentives to encourage larger orders;
- other incentives in return for direct orders at full retail price, when no retail discount given;
- your payment period. What incentives can you offer to those who pay sooner; what penalties to those who take longer?

Promotion

The purpose of promotion is to generate increased profitable sales. Promotion is not another word for public relations; there should be a direct and measurable link between promotion and sales.

Promotional campaigns achieve their desired results by changing and/or directing the attitudes of the target audience: informing and persuading them; managing their conversion from unawareness of the product to repeat purchase; expanding their numbers. This will involve different promotional vehicles at different stages of the marketing process: perhaps a poster early on to shout a simple announcement message, with a more detailed leaflet nearer launch time.

Promotions are aimed at trade customers (stockists), influencers (media, reviewers, opinion shapers such as chat show hosts and style leaders) and end users.

The promotional mix available to this end consists of the following types of activity:

- free (such as public relations);
- paid (such as space advertising);
- point of sale (a sales message where goods are sold);
- informational (such as catalogues, brochures, exhibitions and reps calling);
- motivational (incentive schemes to generate orders; for example, persuading stockists to take more in return for increased discounts, or encouraging consumers to buy through added value offers in mailshots, consumer promotions or competitions).

The coordination of this mix will seek to do the following:

- identify target audience;
- determine the communication objectives;
- decide on the promotional mix;
- select the communication channel;
- assign the total promotional budget;
- design the message;
- decide on the timing;
- forecast the results;
- measure the results;
- take corrective action;
- draw up new forecast and contingency plans.

Place

This involves the physical movement of the goods to be sold: distribution. The following need to be considered:

- warehousing (individual or cooperative?);
- retail outlets (all or some? Should wide availability or exclusivity be built into the product?);
- stocking policy;
- delivery frequency;
- minimum order size; small order surcharges;
- method of delivery;

– use of wholesalers.

These choices will depend on:

– the nature of the customer base (how easy are they to reach and how do they like to buy?);
– the resources of the company (what can you afford?);
– the wider business situation: what other options for getting the product to the consumer do you have (door-to-door sales, party plan and so on)?

For more information see Chapter 7 on distribution.

(Period of) time
Consider:

– seasonal variations in the market-place (will customers want to buy your summer clothes in mid-winter?);
– in-house considerations (when are your slack/busy periods?);
– taking distributor/carrier schedules into account;
– the schedule for exporting.

Profit
The most basic of economies is subsistence. A slight advance on this creates a surplus of revenue which can be used for trade, and should ensure the continued growth of the local economy. Similarly, in business, unless you make a profit, the survival of the product being marketed is questionable; in the longer term your company itself may be threatened. Many firms use a *loss leader* to attract (eg record clubs), but in the long term this is a promotional gambit to gain profitable customers.

Revenue should:

a) cover the costs of the promotion;
b) cover the costs of the product research and production.

Profit is what is left once these costs have been covered, and should contribute to company overheads and future survival.

Long-term and short-term profit aims also need to be compatible: will the short-term need to sell, in order to raise cash, wreck the chances of longer-term, and greater, profitability? (No retail buyer likes to reorder at a higher unit cost than the initial order, although this is often overlooked in the manufacturer's desperation to get into particular types of outlet.)

Profit also needs to be accountable. It must be measured in the different company centres where it originates, and according to life cycle and long-term expectations of different products: general company levels are meaningless unless you know the source.

Finally, there are a few other considerations for the marketing orientated company to master.

Training

Marketing orientated companies regard their staff as one of their most important assets: they train them, motivate them and in return are rewarded with a more stable workforce. This is nothing new. The founder of IBM, Thomas Watson, believed that a company's annual investment in education, training and internal communications should increase at a rate greater than the company's rate of growth.

Even today few companies espouse training to this extent, but the subject is much more positively viewed on all sides of industry. There is a definite movement towards a more qualified workforce, with an emphasis on proven occupational (rather than general educational) competence. Employees have responded by seeing training as a career benefit rather than an implied insult (going 'back to school' inferred that there was more to be learnt). Managements increasingly view training as an on-going, and hence never-ending, process, and one that must be integrated with other motivational and organisational changes in order to be fully effective. (For further consideration, see Chapter 8.)

Flexibility

Marketing orientated companies are flexible; they adapt as market conditions change, having anticipated the way the market is moving.

For example, Clothkits began life as a firm selling packs for home sewing. The garment pieces were printed on to material, and the customer had to make up according to instructions. These kits were sold by direct mail. In the 1980s, with the retail boom, Clothkits opened about 18 shops, mainly in the south-east of England. These shops did well, selling both the kits and, increasingly, their specially designed and colourful own-brand products. The same 'club' feeling enjoyed by those who had bought the original kits was maintained by the new merchandise. With the decline of high street spending in the early 1990s, the shops, although promoting the brand, were not making any money. Clothkits management were able to sell their brand name to mail order specialist Freemans, while continuing to run the shops under licence (although when trading conditions continued to be difficult, they subsequently decided to close them down).

Other product names have been equally stranded by time but continue to serve as the market develops. *Draper's Record* is still the main publication for the rag trade, but ask any 16-year-old where the local draper is and you will probably be looked at with amazement. *Good Housekeeping* has become a sophisticated magazine for women of 35 to 45 plus. I suspect that the fact that the editorial columns refer to the magazine as 'GH' implies that the staff too find the image of a magazine dedicated to nourishing meals rather embarrassing; most of the regular buyers probably no longer even notice.

In other words, as markets change, products must change with them or die. The need for managerial flexibility is demonstrated in several theoretical models, two of which are reproduced below. Both must be prefixed with a health warning.

It has recently been argued that theoretical models such as these are dangerous for two main reasons. First, the matrices confuse 'product' (which may, of course, decline as consumer preferences change) with 'brand' (which if carefully managed will prove far more adaptable and hence durable). (For more on branding see the next chapter.)

Second, it is extremely difficult to decide where a product sits on a matrix at any particular time. New consumer trends can provide revival opportunities for long-established products (breakfast cereals that were high in fibre long before it was popular to make the claim). Topical events can wreck the future prospects of good sellers overnight. (Do you remember the slimming cubes called Ayds? They were hastily renamed.)

Nevertheless, I reproduce these matrices because I believe that they

| | Phase | | | |
	Introduction	Growth	Maturity	Decline
Sales	low	fast growing	slow growth	decline
Profits	negative	rising to peak	decline	low to zero
Cash flow	negative	moderate	high	low
Customer	innovators	mass market	mass market	laggards
Competitors	few	growing	shake out	few

Diagram 1. *Product life cycle*

provide both a useful starting point for thinking about the shifting nature of markets, and a valuable framework for looking objectively at the immediate past of your own company.

Diagram 1 is a matrix revealing how product lifestyle characteristics can change. Just as the marketing orientated company will put a great deal of research and thought into the product created, so the product will appeal to different customers and have a varying profit contribution to the company throughout its life cycle. It is not a constant once created.

Diagram 2 links a product's competitive position with its market attractiveness, to indicate the way in which the marketing orientated company should be viewing its future.

Market attractiveness	Competitive position		
Attractive	Leader	Try harder	Double or quit
Average	Growth	Custodial (holding on)	Phased withdrawal
Unattractive	Cash generation	Phased withdrawal	Disinvest
	Strong	Average	Weak

Diagram 2. *Directional policy matrix*

Chapter 3

The Meaning of Marketing in the Book Trade

Marketing to publishers is what *n'est ce pas* is to the French. A term that means just what the speaker intends, with a specific meaning that is infinitely variable.

(Entry to Horace Bent's competition for a definition of marketing in publishing, *Bookseller*, June 1992)

Having looked at what marketing encompasses in theory, and means to other industries, this chapter will look at whether the broadly accepted scope of marketing can and should be applied to books.

Perhaps the first thing to note is that, as Horace Bent's competition showed, there is no consensus about the meaning of marketing within publishing; it can cover anything from the title of a service department to an entire company philosophy. Deborah Rea of Astron told me that she often starts interviews for marketing jobs by asking what candidates understand by the term; their definitions are similarly wide in scope.

Within some publishing houses, sales, promotions and publicity are subsections of the marketing department; in others, in particular the more literary houses, they are often alternatives, with no supervisory marketing structure at all. Even in firms which do have a dedicated marketing department, its scope and influence can generally be traced to whether the company senior management rose through marketing or editorial routes.

Certainly the book trade press steers clear of covering the 'meaning of marketing' debate engaged in by the professional marketing press. Does this demonstrate our professional sterility or creditable resistance to hype (the theorising of the obvious that arguably all new academic disciplines go through)?

An initial estimate of commitment to marketing

So, when looking at an individual publishing company, how can you tell how fundamental a role marketing plays in the business? Perhaps first by examining the firm in relation to the marketing activity checklist supplied in the previous chapter.

People. How well does the firm understand its market: what kind of people they are; what motivates them; what they aspire to; what they need and how they like to buy? Is any market research being done into how the market is changing; new markets that are developing?

Product. Are books acquired piecemeal or commissioned to meet market needs? Who is on the look-out for new titles? In most companies it will be the commissioning editor, but are these recruitable from the marketing side of the company too, rather than editorial alone? (Good copy editors do not necessarily make good market opportunity spotters.) Are promising manuscript submissions viewed by departments other than editorial? Are they seen as finite, or initial product ideas that must be adapted to meet market needs? Does anybody decide how many titles to publish each year; is this figure stuck to?

Price. How is price established? Is there full consideration of market demand, production equations and company priorities before the price is set? Is it set by editorial or marketing in consultation? Is research done into what the competition are charging/what other product alternatives cost? What is the break-even point at which sales recoup initial costs? What offers/variants to list price are there/can there be?

Promotion. Does each product get a specific promotion plan or is it a case of doing the best you can with the limited time/resources available? Are related products linked in joint promotions? Does the marketing department circulate their plans in-house, and if so at what stage? Is feedback welcome: how much in-house cooperation/antagonism is there? Does the sales information that the company puts out reflect their own or the market's priorities? (Is the copy heavy with company or product details? Are product features or benefits given priority? Is what is new emphasised?)

Place. How well does the company understand where the market is and how best to reach it? How does the market find it most convenient to buy and pay? Are all their buying criteria being met? Might they buy more if they were better provided for? How efficient is the distribution system for getting the product to the selling location?

Period of time. Are promotions planned for times of the year when the market is most likely to be receptive? Are there contingency plans should things go wrong? How are marketing results monitored at various points from the initial effort?

43

Profit. What will be the break-even and eventual profit margins on the product/each promotion? How will profit levels be measured and acted upon? What profit margin must be maintained for the firm to stay in business?

Even such a basic outline of how marketing can be implemented in business will probably make someone with a publishing background feel slightly uncomfortable, conscious as we are of how our industry 'fudges the issues'. Nevertheless, there *are* specific problems that the book trade faces in trying to implement a full marketing orientation. After examining these in more detail I will look at what marketing can do to help deal with them.

What problems does the book trade face in trying to implement a marketing orientation?

1. Tradition
In a frantically busy job, the easiest option, and often the only hope of maintaining some sort of grasp on sanity, is to maintain the status quo. In many publishing houses the sheer weight of tradition ('we have always done things this way'), combined with the great pressure of work from the volume of titles coming through, can make it hard to get around to changing the accepted system. Sir John Harvey-Jones argues that it is now time for a change:

> the best way of avoiding mistakes was by not doing anything, because you were unlikely to get it wrong. That style is quite inappropriate for today and tomorrow.

Sympathy for marketing aims has also been hard to secure, in a largely editorially dominated industry. As John Roberts of BCA commented, editors have often dominated and yet 'editors have tended to make poor chief executives'.

Several houses view themselves as continuing the great literary traditions of those who started the firms. This opinion coalesces nicely with a view of publishing as a moral enterprise rather than just a trade, and thus hovering slightly above the grubby profit-requiring reality of other industries. But looking back, it was not lovers of literature who founded the great houses, but entrepreneurs:

> In fact most successful houses were founded by characters memorable

mainly for their meanness, their ruthlessness towards their authors and their lack of interest in the books they were publishing.

(*Independent on Sunday*, 17 November 1991)

This spirit has continued in publishers' arrogant assumption that everyone else is as pro-book as they are; the enormous degree of familiarity assumed by the book trade on the part of the general public. A pro-book culture is something that all in the trade must try to cultivate, but this starts by not taking it for granted.

One of my favourite props for talks at Book House Training Centre is the front cover from a past edition of the *Bookseller*. It features six faces with the slogan 'you can always recognise a bestselling author'. Really? Out of the six faces I can only recognise one, and no bookseller or publisher of my acquaintance has been able to do much better. A straw poll among a few non-publisher friends revealed that none had any idea who published their favourite author, or could in fact name more than five publishing houses.

2. Over-production

I touched on this in Chapter 1. Every year in Britain more than 5000 new plants are introduced. The grocery business produces around 3500 – 4000 new lines. But for depth of product line, no one beats the publishers.

The total of new products (new books and new editions) in 1992 was 78,835, a 16.4 per cent rise on the 1991 total of 67,704; that is more than 1500 titles a week; 250 a day from Monday to Friday. And the total continues to rise: between 1981 and 1991 the number rose somewhere between 45 per cent (Paul Scherer) and 73 per cent (Dr Frank Fishwick of the Cranfield Institute). The UK's inventory total is 500,000 different titles; each year around 550,000 changes are made to price, status, availability and so on. A medium-sized bookshop will stock 18,000 titles (incidentally about the same number of different products held by a Tesco supermarket) but have access to half a million.

But whereas a bookshop usually offers customer access to *all* the new titles available, a supermarket may decide to launch only around 1000 new products a year, some of which will be replacements or reformulations of existing lines rather than completely new products. Around 95 per cent of supermarket stock is ordered centrally through EPOS feedback (although individual managers may decide to choose certain product lines if they know they will sell well in their local area). The book trade's emphasis on wide availability ('whatever you want, we can order it') is unusual in retailing, as is the degree of cooperation among stockists. What is more, most bookshops will refer customers to another store if the item requested is not held in stock by them; there were reactions of horror within the trade when a memo was leaked from a major chain saying that this was *not* to be the standard practice.

British publishing is proportionately large for the size of the home market. America has a domestic market nearly five times the size of the UK and yet the publishing figures are proportionately smaller. (1991: 110,080; 1990: 104,144. Source: Bowker.)

Within Europe, the UK currently publishes the highest number of titles of any of the five largest European countries. (*NB*: for comparison purposes the following figures are based on 1991 publishing totals.)

	No of books pa 1991[1]	Population (millions)[2]	Books per head pa	Spending on books per head pa[1]
UK	68,350	56	.00122	£44.00
Germany	56,400	79	.00071	£60.00
Spain	43,900	39	.00113	£47.00
France	39,500	57	.00069	£39.50
Italy	34,500	58	.00059	£28.00

Sources: 1. Datamonitor, from *European Book Publishing* 1992; 2. *Whitaker's Almanac* 1993 (1992 figures).

The number of titles published in the UK has grown particularly strongly since 1988, and overtook Germany, its closest rival, in 1989. Interestingly, title production has fallen in Germany since a peak in 1988, despite the increased requirements for books after reunification. It seems that the trend has been towards the sale of existing books, with high demand coming from the East, rather than the production of new works. But the Germans are also the highest spenders on books in Europe, spending an average of £60 per head on books every year, and the Spanish (at £47 per head) spend more than the British (£44). The number of titles produced per annum is rising fastest in Italy.

It is worth noting here that the figures on spending per head above show a similar trend to those revealed in a worldwide survey produced by Euromonitor in 1990. This put expenditure on books in the UK eleventh, at £34 per head – behind Germany (£66), Norway (£64), Finland (£53), Sweden (£53), USA (£50), Switzerland (£44), Denmark (£38), Spain (£36), France (£35) and Canada (£34).

How did this over-production arise?

- Because of the momentum of existing levels of publishing. To quote Magnus Magnusson, the spirit of 'I've started so I'll finish'.

- English is an international language, and the UK has long been the centre of English language publishing. Many overseas houses have a foothold here; for example, the German giant Springer Verlag publishes 900 titles a year, of which 600 are in English. Several of the great growth areas of publishing in recent years are UK based: ELT, academic publishing, and American and other overseas imports (mostly produced by the exporting branches of American academic institutions, as well as a handful of well-established British academic firms).

- The UK has wide international markets, and a much higher export ratio than the USA.

- Proponents of the NBA argue that resale price maintenance in the UK means that less emphasis is placed on block-busting bestsellers than in the USA. But the UK's 'output far outstrips those of other European countries with more rigid price regimes' (Dr Frank Fishwick, *Bookseller*, 21 February 1992).

Does it matter?

> Oversupply of product is one of the main causes of financial inefficiency in the book business.
>
> (John Brown, *Viz*; interview in *Bookseller* 25 May 1990)

Is the immense output of UK publishers important? Or is it another example of the great British talking point, like the Royal family or national sports teams? People talk about it but no one does anything about it. The industry cooperates internally to manage the huge volume, through the ISBN and bar-coding. BML has shown that both demand and regard for books have held up well during the recession, so once things recover, will the wide book choice available mean that the market will pick up again quickly?

Yes, it does matter

I would argue that over-production does matter, because demand has failed to grow with publishing output; there is 'a greater number of goods chasing demand that refuses to grow concomitantly' (Stephen Adamson, letter to the *Bookseller*, 20 September 1991).

Over the past few years the total value of home sales has risen only slightly more than inflation, so in terms of units sold there has been a slight decline. Continuing the high production levels has only avoided disaster because books have become cheaper to produce.

Cheaper production methods meant that the market could go two ways: produce the same number of books for less money, and cut overheads to match, or produce more books for the same money. Cutting overheads, including staff loss, or considering a merger to gain economies of scale, are much more painful and far-reaching processes, and as competitors produced more and stole market share everyone else followed suit.

Over-production also matters because the market has changed. Many of the UK's old colonial markets are buying much less from us; new independent governments prefer a home-grown product which at the same time promotes cultural nationalism. Economic weakness in other countries means that they can afford to buy less, and meanwhile the challenge from the Americas, also publishing in English, has grown. Some have commented that over-production means that both editorial and production standards have fallen.

Ultimately, like so many other dilemmas in the publishing industry, this is a situation in which individual houses must lead the way. In 1991 there were substantial attempts to reduce overheads in the trade. There were staff losses – Paul Scherer estimated that 5 per cent of *all* publishing jobs were eliminated in that year – and many employers jumped on the bandwagon once others started it rolling. As part of this rethink, several firms have vowed to publish less, others have backed up intention with an indication of scale. For example, the Penguin Group published 20 per cent fewer titles in 1992 than in 1989; Faber too have made a commitment to 20 per cent fewer than 1990 by 1993. Gail Rebuck said that Random House will be publishing around 25 per cent fewer titles in 1993. Paul Scherer related title production at Transworld very tightly to staffing levels: with a total of 190 staff the company can produce around 100 hardbacks and 500 paperbacks a year and then 'give the attention to each book that is needed'.

Looking ahead, what are the long-term results of producing fewer books? For authors of general fiction the main problem will be getting published. With a noticeable decline in hardback fiction, the 'strong are getting stronger while new authors are being squeezed out' (*Bookwatch*, compilers of the bestseller list for the *Bookseller*, 1 February 1992). There has been a marked tendency to try to create writers out of 'television personalities' or other well-known characters, providing a ghost writer if necessary. (Would-be authors of fiction might do better to switch to non-fiction, especially on niche subjects. There seems to be a burgeoning of small specialised publishing companies looking for just such talent without the accompanying, and expensive, 'name' to go with it.)

3. Publishing as a product-driven industry

The fundamental problem of publishing is that it's not market led, it's supply led. We generally try to find a market after we publish.

(John Brown, *Viz*, interview in the *Bookseller*, 25 May 1990)

Allied to the problem of too many books being produced is the one of which books to publish. The main issue here is whether or not a marketing rationale is used as the basis for taking on titles in the first place, not just in deciding how to sell them once they are 'in-house'. Do you commission the books that meet specific market needs, or go for the titles that turn up at the front door and shout 'publish me!'? Traditionally, the industry has been bad at distinguishing between the two.

Similarly, in the past many publishing houses have seemed unable to assess the respective merits of the various types of book they were publishing (including the crucial categories of those which would ultimately be profitable and those which would not). All publishers' lists are likely to contain the following:

- yesterday's money-makers;
- today's money-makers;
- tomorrow's money-makers;
- long-term developments;
- sleepers;
- management vanities;
- failures.

But there was often insufficient emphasis placed on distinguishing between them. Publishers were often unwilling to accept their own, in-house, market research such as sales statistics and feedback from reps. All titles will not do equally well, even if awarded identical budgets. Back the winners with additional spending – don't throw more money after losers in the hope that they will make up the gap. In other words, all books are *not* born equal.

Publishing firms today are, however, learning how to manage the in-house and out of house reporting facilities better, to find out precisely what is going on in the market, and hence make logical decisions about which titles to publish. Many publishers have for some time had in-house computer monitoring of orders, information captured at order processing stage. Now wholesalers and retailers too have the technology to identify, with accuracy, the source of their sales. Likewise, bookshops with computers are able to work out the specific economies of selling: turnover per square foot; per employee; per season; gross margin and stock turn.

Allied to the problem of which titles to publish has been a poor under-

49

standing of the nature of the competition. And by competition, I don't just mean other books. The realisation that books compete not just with other books, but with a whole range of other information sources and leisure spends, has come late, and is a direct result of the industry's over-concentration on products rather than markets.

For example, for the first time in December 1992, *The Guinness Book of Records* was not in the Christmas bestseller list. The main reason put forward for this was the rise of Nintendo Game Boys. Bought for the same market, they took spending away from books. Similarly, in recent years there has been a huge growth in video sales (1985 turnover was about £15 million; in 1991 it was estimated at around £400 million and to be poised to overtake the video rental market). Videos sell to similar market profiles to book buyers. and those publishers who see themselves in the communication business rather than the book business are dipping their toe in, often having been successful in audio-tape product extensions. For the same reason, many traditional bookshops are starting to sell videos. (See also Chapter 6 on market research.)

4. Inadequate financial structures

There has always been a low threshold for commercial success in the book trade, much more so than in other industries. It is possible to exist at much lower levels of commercial activity than other businesses, to sell relatively few and still break even.

The record market (across all the various formats) was valued at around £1.25 billion in the UK in 1991 (the UK book trade was worth roughly £1.5 billion at the same time), yet for the former a 'bestseller' is about 2 million, for the latter around 150,000. Similarly, selling 2000 medium-priced boxes of chocolates, of a new brand design, developed by a major confectioner, would be judged a complete disaster given the hugh amounts of investment needed before such a product is launched. (Cadbury-Schweppes recently invested £7 million in a new factory and £5 million in a marketing campaign to launch their new chocolate bar, *Time Out*.) Selling 2000 copies of a new novel by an up-and-coming writer, at a similar purchase price to the box of chocolates, would be judged a success, taking the longer-term view of future promise and ownership of rights.

A traditional view has prevailed of bookselling: a nice job for the civilised but semi-retired (whether as a result of supplementary income or advancing age). A job that involved selling, certainly, but with the promotion of a worthy product no 'hard sell' was needed; more the enjoyable responsibility of recommending to friends (hence many booksellers' genuine distaste for books of the Wicked Willy or Madonna variety). More emphasis was often placed on the skills of classification than of spotting market opportunities. Low pay for assistants was compensated for by the general satisfaction of working with books. In particularly specialised arms of the trade, wider objectives supplemented or replaced the need for even lowish levels of profit. For example, there are 500 – 600 Christian bookshops in the UK, but individual turnover rarely exceeds £50,000 pa.

It has proved difficult to break the 'subsistence' mentality in the industry; it was easier to get on with the volume of publishing than rethink a company's financial aims and structures. This meant that when the market-place altered, firms were badly structured to survive.

What changed? First, the book trade's traditional balance of power was fundamentally altered by the emergence of strong chains of booksellers endowed with appropriate levels of buying power.

> Ten years ago the publishing industry dominated the market and booksellers were totally subservient; now there is a real balance of power. The book market has grown up and can fight its corner.
>
> (Tim Waterstone, quoted in the *Guardian*, 20 March 1991)

Second, for general trade publishers, the position of the bestselling author changed. Whereas Joseph Conrad had to sell the copyright of his works to his publisher/bookseller before he got into print, in the late 1980s there was a sudden and great change in the balance of power between bestselling author and publisher, a vast increase in the former's selling power. Spiralling advances and 'cheque-book publishing' followed, with firms paying 'more to keep their book away from a rival publisher than to reflect its realistic bottom-line potential' (Tim Waterstone). These authors too often felt alienated by the large conglomerates that emerged; there was an accompanying 'ethos, where authors go for all they can get because they have nothing to lose in terms of relationships' (Tim Rix).

But these shifts were imposed on top of traditional financial structures. Excessive advances were being paid by firms, but the titles they published were not bringing in any more than they had always done. There was immense pressure to sell the lead titles, but many did not earn out their advances. Many companies were supported by high borrowings – bad news when interest rates rose sharply at the start of the recession. Nigel Newton of Bloomsbury summed the situation up as a 'lack of financial discipline' (*Independent on Sunday*, 17 November 1991).

5. Inappropriate management structures

Many aspects of internal company organisation were accentuated by poor financial handling, both in terms of company management structure and day-to-day decision making.

Structure

Anticipated economies of scale, often the rationale for unions of firms, often proved illusory: genuine overlapping interests were what saved money, not amalgamations *per se*. The situation was made worse by other aspects of inadequate management structure: poor distribution; the waste of returns; increasing the workload of staff with extra lists that required different targeting from their existing responsibilities.

Most publishing companies were slow to computerise, although those which did found considerable savings were to be made from, for example, installing desk top publishing or accepting manuscripts in machine readable format.

In-house management

Management training has never had a high priority in most publishing houses. And while you can learn editorial skills as a secretary while watching and helping your editor boss, structured management skills are more difficult to acquire in this way. In difficult times, the results of this became more obvious.

6. The recession

After the shopping boom of the mid 1980s, driven by high levels of consumer credit, recession hit the high street in the last years of the decade. There were many problems:

– The constraints of belonging to the ERM, and then our sudden departure, affected sterling. Slower, if more stable, rates of economic growth now seem more likely.

– The rising costs of operating on the high street began to squeeze margins; business rateable values rose dramatically, and so therefore did rents. Many property agreements were subject to 'upward only' rent reviews, inappropriate when trading conditions later proved so difficult. Even for those businesses owning their own premises, mortgage interest rates shot up. To protect themselves, booksellers demanded higher discounts and extended discount periods, but only the larger chains could enforce these wishes. Banks too sought to limit their exposure to risk from loans that they had previously offered easily, making life unpredictable for new and growing businesses. For example, at the end of 1991 the Midland Bank suddenly called in 50 per cent of the loan that provided the working capital for the newly independent Phoenix Bookshops.

- The structural imbalance of the market: there were too many shops chasing too few sales. High interest rates led to falling consumer spending; only the retailers of products for which there is a stable demand (mainly food) were largely protected from downturn. Arthur Young suggested that 200 – 300 bookshops will close by 1996.

- The changing nature of consumer demand: more price conscious; more ethical; plus the requirements of an ageing population.

- Reduced public spending. According to Book Trust, book buying by public libraries declined during the 1980s by one-third, a substantial loss of what was previously a steady income for non-bestsellers. School spending was also down, whatever is claimed about 'real terms'.

But these are general market problems, not specific to the publishing industry. And while there have been bookshop closures, BA membership has been buoyed up by new firms joining. The total value of expenditure on books has in fact held up well during the recession, and most economists point to books holding on to a larger than average market share in the immediate future. (The Henley Centre for Forecasting has predicted 1.7 per cent growth in consumer spending on books in 1993, and between 2 and 3 per cent between 1994 and 1997. Euromonitor and Mintel have suggested similar figures.)

Ultimately, the same applies to the book trade as any other industry: a more complex examination of the financial realities of running a business is necessary, in these difficult trading conditions, than was perhaps the case in the past.

The implementation of marketing strategies in publishing

So, given the specific differences and problems of the book industry, is it possible fully to employ marketing? Must the book industry change, and if so how? Is it capable of change? If so, what are the implications for the future of publishing?

It is important to say straightaway that the development of marketing, as a primary driving force in large publishing environments, *is happening*. The best companies today – Reed, Transworld, Headline, Dorling Kindersley, Walker and so on – are all marketing driven. These firms are not alone in being able to spot a potential market but, crucially, they excel at managing its development. All have strong leadership, and the companies have been built rather than being the product of piecemeal additions; they are strong and stable professional organisations, established to last. Clear in their objectives, free from short-term experiments, they understand their markets and are good at contacting them. They reach out to consumers with special sales techniques and organisation, and expand the market for books:

> Our list is determinedly commercial. For the industry to prosper it has to make a clearer connection between what it takes on and what the public wants.
>
> (Tim Hely Hutchinson quoted in the *Independent*, early 1993)

It is interesting that the general opinion in the trade was confirmed by a recent Society of Authors survey; the same names kept cropping up. Authors, too, like the new professionalism and being kept informed. (Headline, for example, provide them with *monthly* sales figures.)

In many of these companies there is also a new balance of power, taking full account of the importance of marketing in publishing. Most of these firms are marketing, rather than editorial, led, and this means that in-house priorities are different. No longer do marketing departments tend to hear of titles for the first time when they are told how many thousand they must sell. Often they are involved in deciding how big the market is before the project is taken on. Equally significant, there are more ex-industry appointments being made – mostly on the marketing side – proving that experience in selling a product other than books *is* relevant to publishing.

Examples of marketing in action in publishing

Again I will use the seven P formula from the previous chapter (see page 34) to give examples of what is going on in the industry.

People

Marketing tries to identify customer segments and sell to them, all the while considering the diverse nature of customer needs. Thus one book can be variously entertainment, education, status, a keepsake or perhaps augment another product as in the 'book of the film'. Equally, people with otherwise similar backgrounds can buy wide ranges of texts because they are looking for different satisfactions from their various purchases.

The way this has been most notably achieved in the book world is through *specialisation*. As we have seen, the spate of amalgamations in the late 1980s did not, in many cases, bring economies of scale. Specialisation has proved a far more valuable marketing tool in developing a business, particularly during the recession.

> The Next/Habitat lifestyle mould of retailing is finished. The 90s will be the decade of specialisation, of targeted retailers offering something new and radical: service and choice.
>
> (Martin Grindley, *Bookseller*, 19 April 1991)

> The most successful companies currently are those strong in the international publication of professional, academic and reference books. The hardest hit companies have been those devoted to publishing general books for the home market.
>
> (Stewart Binnie, venture capitalist, *Bookseller*, 22 November 1991)

This specialisation is going on in all sectors of business, not just publishing. Direct mailings are getting smaller and more targeted; increased use of telemarketing and selling through new locations is replacing blanket press and television campaigns (the latter in an attempt to combat 'zapping' before commercial breaks). Hence, the media campaign that only the foolish stop advertising in a recession – they have not stopped, just switched to a more precise vehicle. This trend is to be seen worldwide, abetted by computers which first made it all possible, and then became more affordable to smaller specialist businesses who could profit from the new opportunities.

Specialist retailers are emerging and thriving. But it is important to recognise straightaway that specialist does not necessarily equal small. Toys 'Я' Us has been in the UK for only seven years, but in that time the company has seized around 33 per cent of the toy sale market, leading to the demise of many smaller independent general toyshops. Likewise, one can point to the expansion of other market specialists – the Swedish furniture store IKEA, and PC World. The Pentos Group includes other specialist brand name stores besides Dillons: Athena prints and posters; Ryman the stationer, and office equipment and furniture supplier Wilding Office Systems.

The retail market-place for books has changed dramatically in recent years, with the emergence of large chains of specialist booksellers. In 1984 six main bookselling groups in the UK had between them 397,000 square feet of selling space. This rose to 945,000 in 1988, a rise from 114 bookshops to 263, and all, it should be noted, developed with fewer problems than on the publishing side of the business. Specialist bookshops, stocking in depth, continue to do well, claiming vast increases in profits. The major chains claim that they grew between 5 and 12 per cent in 1989 – 1990;

Pentos said their sales were up 22 per cent in 1990. Wholesalers, too, say they are doing well.

In some cases the expansion of the chain bookshop in an area already well served by local bookshops has led to the closure of smaller rivals – the 'category killer', as seen in Hampstead. Interestingly, in Germany it has been found that smaller, and more established, bookshops can survive when chain stores arrive, despite a temporary drop when a new store opens, particularly if they offer something extra: service; product knowledge, and a wide and sensible choice of stock.

But prosperity is not the preserve of the larger firms: smaller specialist businesses are thriving in the UK too, and the category of specialist bookshops is growing, as evinced by the growing numbers listed in the *Directory of Specialist Bookdealers in the UK* (Peter Marcan Publications). These shops not only specialise in books, they take their specialisation further.

For example, the Silver Moon Women's Bookshop in the Charing Cross Road has doubled the size of its premises and is expanding fast. Their gross profit margin is around 37 per cent with few returns. They put this success down to being specialist feminist/women's book suppliers who know their market and offer an excellent service.

> I have a nightmare. It is that Dillons *et al.* will suddenly start offering service. I remember Frank Brazier (of Pentos) saying at the BA Conference in Cardiff in 1992 that his primary concern was for his shareholders. Well ours is for our customers, and I think that is the right way round.
>
> (Jane Cholmeley, Silver Moon Women's Bookshop)

On the other side of the road there is a bookshop specialising in crime and murder titles, Murder One. Stanfords of Long Acre continue to offer a specialist map and travel guide book service, dealing with, if advertising bookings in the *Bookseller* are anything to go by, one of the most competitive sectors of British publishing. Computer books provide the highest profit per linear foot in the trade and make up one of the highest growth potentials in the book business. BML's *Books and the Consumer* survey found that, of all practical reference books, computer manuals are bought at the highest rate of all major subject areas (currently three to four a year, up from about two in 1989). Consequently, shops specialising in them are doing well – whether with a section or a dedicated store such as the PC Bookshop in London. All these businesses benefit from strong customer loyalty – for they are meeting customer needs – and supplement sales to calling customers with sales to their mailing lists.

Other shops which do well are responsive to market conditions and flexible in response; they know their market and understand how they want to buy. Hoopers of Harborne in Birmingham made a deliberate decision to complement mass market retailers in the city rather than compete; they find the intimacy of their shop is preferred to more impersonal city centre sites. The proprietor, Jane Hooper, finds that the public respond well to a specialist bookshop that takes the trouble to get to know customers and fulfil their needs, and that customers are not intimidated about asking for help as they are in the larger stores. Tracking down individual titles can be like working as a detective, and provides immense satisfaction as well as a loyal customer base. The real worry is that margins on books are low while overheads, principally rent, are enormous.

Hoopers also sells greetings cards, and other shops too are offering similar products, or perhaps cups of coffee – items which are compatible with the sale of books but which offer higher profit margins. Other moves towards a more diverse stock may offer different benefits. The profit margins on videos are lower than books, but the stock turn in general is quicker. Similarly, profit margins on stationery items are in general lower, and the market may be particularly competitive for branded products, but stocking such items may bring new customers into the shop, as well as providing existing customers with another pretext for a visit. Children's book clubs too have experimented with cross merchandising, and find it adds variety to their packages and widens the appeal of introductory offers. Both BCA and the Red House Book Club do well with selling toys and stationery; both types of merchandise that have profit margins significantly *lower* than books. (In addition to lower discounts, not only are both categories subject to VAT, but toys imported from the Far East are subject to a 9 per cent import duty.)

Smaller UK publishers have emerged to specialise too, a pattern that has been visible in the USA for some time. Richard Abel pointed out that:

> while the buyouts, amalgamations and conglomerations have been going on, a virtually unheralded, scarcely noticed and seldom remarked parallel movement has occurred – a rapid proliferation of small book publishers with turnovers up to $5 million.
>
> (*Bookseller*, 14 September 1990)

As proof of this he cited the number of firms applying for a block of ISBNs each year (increase every year apart from 1974) and more applications occurred when the most amalgamations were going on. Such firms can produce exactly the right type of book for the current economic climate:

> What does sell well in a recession is any decent self-help informational book, from gardening to cookery.
>
> (Graham Lord, *Daily Telegraph*, 4 January 1993)

These are titles for which big, and expensive, author names are not required.

Product

A marketing approach to product development considers the market before producing the product. As we have already seen, general publishing is primarily a product-driven industry, tending to look for the most likely market once the product has been both commissioned and produced.

But when specialist publishers have gone out and created a product to meet market needs they have often been rewarded. For example, back in the 1970s Ginn marketed a single product to meet a vast market – their *English 360* for the teaching of reading in primary schools. It had been developed first in America, then in Australia, and was later carefully revised for the British market. They embarked on a similar exercise in the primary mathematics market, and were tremendously successful because much of the rest of the market was still acquiring books piecemeal rather than looking for specific opportunities, investing and then exploiting them. Today their example is emulated by other market specialists who research and develop long-term products that bring in the profits. These products often also serve to subsidise the more glamorous books produced by the same house; one-off gambles that may or may not work.

> Not surprisingly, toilers in the hidden nine-tenths of the publishing iceberg get fed up at being treated as 'cash-cows' – it is said that there was particular resentment among dictionary makers at HarperCollins over the size of some of the advances being paid by the trade division.
> (Nicholas Faith, financial journalist writing in *The Author*, Spring 1993)

In considering how marketing could be most effectively applied to product development I am going to take just one issue, greatly used in the world of product development outside publishing, but hardly used within it – branding.

The chances are that you do not know who manufactures your favourite washing powder or toothpaste. You probably buy on brand name and reputation rather than manufacturer name. (Unless, of course, you are buying own-brand goods in a supermarket, in which case you are buying their reputation and price benefit as a brand in its own right. Incidentally, Marks & Spencer's carrier bags have probably done more to make the term 'brand name' familiar to the general public than anything else!) The book trade, on the other hand, with vastly more products to deal with, classifies its wares largely on the basis of in-house information.

In a record shop you can search for a particular artist alphabetically by surname; you can see what the fastest selling items are at a glance (they are laid out in the top ten slots) and buy with confidence. Ask in a wine merchant or supermarket for a specific product and you will be told whether or not it is stocked in that particular store (and frequently recommended an alternative if it is not). Do the same in bookshops, and before staff try to track the title you will usually be asked to name the publisher, or even worse the imprint (the what?). Of course, the publishers' system is primarily a function of the need to manage the huge number of titles available, but the trade still expects a vastly more informed public than other manufacturers.

Most customers could not care less who publishes a book; it is the author, and sometimes the look of the imprint, that they remember. Perhaps the most fast-growing brand in publishing of late has been the name, and reputation, of the bookshop/book chain. Retailers have segmented the market, recognising that customers are not all the same and have differing wants and needs. For example, Waterstones like to appear quite up-market; their shops are staffed in the main by graduates who know, and enthuse about, books. Dillons are presented as more mass market and street-wise, the consumer's friend who targets price fixing and offers customers the best deal. Volume One bookshops go for a brighter, brasher image than was traditional in British bookselling. Britain's biggest 'book supermarket', launched by Colin Sullivan in January 1993 at Victoria Station, was unashamedly brash in appearance, with neon lighting and vast red-on-white bargain signs hanging above the piles of remaindered books stacked on tables. 'We are trying to make bookselling less snobbish, that's why we called the new shop a shed,' commented Mr Sullivan. But unfortunately, non-adherence to traditional practice included non-payment of suppliers, and the business was in trouble by the end of February.

Some publishers feel that this growing bookshop branding has been at the expense of the acceptance of individual publisher-branded promotions, which are seen as diluting the bookshop message. Meanwhile, the independents could do more collectively to promote what amounts to their own brand – choice, experience and product knowledge.

What are brands?

A food company develops a new type of snack. Having thought of a name for the product, their first action will probably be to register it as a brand, or trademark, so that the exact specifications cannot be replicated by competitors. There are 250,000 trademarks in the UK, three million in Europe, one million in the USA and another million in Japan. And it has been estimated that 18 out of every 20 new brands fail.

Branding strives for memorability. Brands summarise what the customer can expect from a product: value, consistency, permanence and reassurance. Some companies try to anticipate public tastes and interests with a distinctive brand, others attempt to join the market area of a successful brand with a 'me too' product. Once one brand is successfully established, variants (or 'extensions') can be launched to generate more sales (eg different flavours of the Yorkie bar were introduced once the solid chocolate one was successful; Persil is available in different strengths and formats, drawing on the success of the brand name soap powder).

Brands can also prove extremely durable. Successfully managed, they can be adapted to changing market conditions so that the product of today, although identified by the same brand name, bears little resemblance to the original manufacturer's specification. Think of the transformation in car engines over the years; today's leading brands are usually the longest established names. Ford's Model T is in museums but the company brand name lives on.

And as durable products with established markets, brands can form extremely important company assets, part of a company's intellectual property; hence recent discussions about how firms can include brand value on the balance sheet and so see it reflected in share price, or use brand value as additional security for loans. Brands certainly have promoted mergers and acquisitions, even in publishing. Rupert Murdoch's HarperCollins bought Unwin Hyman in 1990. Humphrey Carpenter suggested that one particular brand attracted his interest:

> Mr Murdoch seems to have liked the idea of publishing Tolkien, but to be interested in nothing else on the Unwin Hyman list.
>
> (*Daily Telegraph*, 9 January 1991)

Branding and the publishing industry

There are relatively few meaningful brands in publishing. Ask someone in the street what a penguin is and the chances are they will say either a chocolate biscuit or a paperback book (hence the company's strong objections when Benson and Hedges used the bird in cigarette advertisements). There are few other book trade brands equally well known to the general public.

Other publishing brands are identifiable because of the format of the book, without the name of the company necessarily being known (for example, Virago green; Mills and Boon pink; Faber design; Ladybird hardbacks and Dorling Kindersley cut-outs on a white background – hence, in part, their success in launching stores within stores). Some authors are brands in their own right: people will buy the next Jeffrey Archer,

P D James or Ken Follett because they enjoyed the last one, and this is brand loyalty (hence the confusion engendered in the public mind when the cousins' books were formatted in exactly the same way). The Mrs Beeton brand name continues to sell cookery books whose content bears little relation to that of the originals, other than the general principles of comprehensiveness and practicality. And there are some brands that transcend publishing through multi-media deals: Thomas the Tank Engine and Peter Rabbit.

Many publishing companies confuse brand with company name: the only unifying factor they can see when every book is different. Thus to a publisher, the new autumn list may constitute a brand. A bookseller, on the other hand, will see the list not as a whole, but as a collection of individual titles; each author as a brand, or as the basis for a cross-publisher group (eg new books about the Prime Minister; Booker short-list novels; major biographies receiving lots of promotion in the run up to Christmas, and hence worth featuring face up at the front of the shop). Thematic promotions from individual publishers may attract attention as a ready-made brand (eg books on China; titles on cake decorating), and hence worthy of in-store promotion, because they provide depth of coverage rather than one-off titles.

There is room for more market research into the meaning of branding in publishing and its value to the industry, and almost certainly into the loss of certain brands, however dear they are in-house, because they mean little to the general public who are meant to be influenced by them. (For example, Vintage abandoned their imprint Sigma, because they felt it was insufficiently recognised.)

In the specialist market (eg academic and scientific) there are difficulties, as it is obviously the author's qualifications to write the book that are important to the customer, not the publisher's name. But a growing (and positive) reputation as a particular type of publisher constitutes an ascendant brand. In the popular market, the publishing industry could also benefit from the market research industry's studies of markets where there are only marginal, or frequently no actual, product differences. An understanding of how consumers relate to, and choose, brands in these circumstances is relevant – the impact of packaging, distribution, pricing and so on. Bloomsbury tried this with a promotion of 'if you enjoyed x, you'll enjoy y' for their own guides to good reading, a concept also found to be popular with the library fiction promotion scheme Well Worth Reading.

Price

Marketing strives to produce a price that is attractive to the market, encourages customers to buy and hence ensures the company's future survival.

But so often, if price is mentioned in the book trade, one of two things happens. Either the arguments for and against the Net Book Agreement are quickly marshalled (price is explained purely in terms of with or without discount), or an impassioned defence of/attack on the prices that publishers charge for books is mounted. Either way, the principal selling point for the trade, that of the tremendous value that books provide, is completely lost. I'll be looking at the NBA in the next chapter, and would like to concentrate here on the issue of value.

> books are not overpriced, they are undervalued
> (Anne Dolamore, letter to the *Bookseller*, 21 January 1992)

Books are good value for money, as anyone who compares the costs of other forms of entertainment, or information access, must surely agree. One paperback equates with less than the cost of cinema entrance, is around the same price as a round of drinks, yet lasts considerably longer. One paperback book costs about the same as four individually packaged birthday cards, and when it comes to comparing the respective amounts of words, design and mental effort that have gone into each product, there really is no comparison.

What is more, books are even better value than they used to be. In 1951, Alexander Macmillan claims, the hardback price of a serious biography or a literary novel could have bought two tickets in the stalls of a West End theatre or dinner for two in a respectable restaurant!

> The equivalent book is now £14.99 whereas the two stalls tickets will cost more than £30 and a comparable dinner about £40.00.
> (*Bookseller*, 20 September 1991)

When that cover price is divided up into component parts payable for royalty and different services, such as warehousing, production and distribution, the percentage left to the publisher seems small. As Tessa Youell, a self-published author commented:

> I'm already wondering how any publisher makes money. Between 35 and 40 per cent of the cover price goes to the bookshops, while 25 per cent of what's left goes to the distributor.

Yet is this message getting across? In marketing terms, 'value for money' is determined by the perceptions of consumers – if they think any book is expensive, as far as they are concerned, it is. Yet the letters page in the *Bookseller* often features extremely articulate complaints from independent booksellers about the price of books. Publishers respond with detailed descriptions of the high costs that they face. Is this defensive attitude missing the point? Are we needlessly obsessed with keeping prices as low as possible? As Richard Charkin wrote on price:

> One extraordinary thing about the British book business is that we spend time and effort debating something which everyone else in the world stopped debating years ago.
>
> (*Bookseller*, 1 May 1992)

The *Books and the Consumer* survey has shown that the general public regard books, for the most part, as very or fairly good value (see Chapter 6). What is more, despite high street gloom during the late 1980s and early 1990s, books have proved fairly recession proof, in particular children's titles.

The price of books in the UK in general keeps pace with the price of other goods: since 1981 the RPI has increased by 54 per cent, the price of general books by 57 per cent (letter from Malcolm Gibson in the *Bookseller*, 20 September 1991). It is true that books are cheaper in the USA but print runs for the larger domestic market are longer, quality is less good (cheaper quality paper, narrow gutters and margins), and the cost of living there, too, is lower.

Books also look worthy of value, hence the great potential for them as gifts highlighted by various market surveys; if you are giving something as a gift you want it to look expensive. Sally Butcher, director of the London-based promotions agency KLP, commented that she liked to use books as promotional items because their 'perceived value by the public is high'. In Australia, where there has been no resale price maintenance for 20 years, Michael Zifcak commented that books were frequently used as promotional items in supermarkets. This was not because the superstores had any ambitions to be serious booksellers, but because 'books are one of the very few commodities with recognisable recommended prices, thereby lending themselves to "two-price" promotion'.

At the upper end of the market, Joanna Mackle of Faber commented that the market for their quality paperbacks was not particularly price sensitive. Waterstones' experience of the top end of the American market, through their new store in Boston, is similar: price is less important than choice, service and product knowledge. Tim Hely Hutchinson similarly commented that quality, design and marketing have more effect on sales than price. Trevor Glover of Penguin said that motivating the public to buy and read is more important than price:

> you need to be able to persuade someone to read [a book] because of

its content – to match the book with the reader. It will be that, not price, that makes a reader invest hours of his or her life with a book.

(*Bookseller*, 1 May 1992)·

How to do this is, of course, much more complicated than focusing on price alone. But is it best done by the trade as a whole, in concerted action? Or, as Richard Charkin claims, is it true that:

generic advertising campaigns, stressing nebulous concepts such as good value for money rarely work. Advertising has to be specific.

Whether individually or collectively, the issue of value instead of price is clearly worth further consideration.

Promotion

A marketing approach to a promotional campaign will stress the benefits to the market that the market finds most convincing; the ones that are needed in order to make a buying decision.

For example, in the increasingly acrimonious battle between Cassells (for Mrs Beeton) and BBC Books (for Delia Smith), mainly waged in trade advertisements in the *Bookseller*, both parties stressed the benefits of their books to the trade. These advertisements talked about sales record, consumer confidence, profit and incentives, and not, as is often the case in publishing promotions, in-house factors (such as extent, information on the company, or irrelevant information about the author).

Place

The selling location

When trading conditions are hard, both manufacturers and retailers must think seriously about how their customers find it most convenient to buy. This includes considering the sales location. Traditionally, far more *angst* has gone into considering how long it takes to get books to bookshops than thinking about where the public might find it most convenient to buy. This situation continues. The retail book trade debates the merits of traditional/non-traditional routes, while many of the sales outlets dubbed non-traditional have a long history (after all Penguins were first sold through Woolworths). And meanwhile other players are exploring and developing new locations for the sale of books almost daily.

So, going back to the customer in the centre of the marketing equation, how right has the trade got it? I plan to look at the subject in two ways: first, a brief resumé of the arguments about where books should be sold, and second, a look at the practicalities to be considered by those thinking about extending the type of outlets through which they sell.

1. Where should books be sold?
In the beginning, booksellers both produced and sold books. The first specialist publishers grew up as their offshoots. Later independent publishers sold their wares to booksellers, and the balance of power in the trade started to move the publishers' way.

But of late many publishers have increasingly felt that the whole market was not being covered by booksellers, either as a matter of course:

> no reasonable bookseller would claim to reach every part of the market or claim to be the only or most effective way of doing so
>
> (Peter Kindersley, letter to the *Bookseller*, 15 May 1992)

or through lack of sufficiently developed marketing awareness on the part of the retail trade. Meanwhile, the demise of the wholesaler Bookwise, which had high penetration of the confectioner, tobacconist, newsagent (CTN) market, has deprived the trade of high sales at the popular end of the market (orders from Bookwise for 100,000 – 150,000 copies of mass market paperbacks were common and are sorely missed).

As a direct consequence of these factors, many publishers felt that there were new ways of reaching potential buyers, and they started either to approach the market directly themselves, or to do so through new outlets. Book clubs, school fairs, bargain bookshops, direct marketing to end users and so on have now been with us for, in some cases, many years, and they work, but still tend to be dubbed 'non-traditional'.

It is worth noting at this point that these developments echo what is going on in society in general. Some of the fastest growing sales outlets for all products in the 1980s have been non-traditional, such as car boot sales, mail order catalogues, exhibitions and fairs, clubs and party selling. Whether or not these non-traditional venues are appropriate vehicles for the sale of books depends on one of two views.

View 1: they expand the market
First, they create extra sales from those who, for whatever reason, do not buy from bookshops. Titles advertised in bookclubs are then asked for in bookshops, and publishers who have tracked the success of titles sold through supermarkets find that there is a strong link with subsequent bookshop sales of other books by the same authors, ie new readers are coming back for more. More exposure produces more sales for everyone.

Second, and more nebulously, these new outlets promote books as general items of appeal, like any other products on which consumers may decide to spend their money (rather than as élitist products for which a measure of both confidence and competence are required before purchase). More promotion through more types of outlet expands public confidence in books, directing spending towards books and away from other non-book products that compete with them. For example, many argue that the development of bargain bookshops is not stealing market share from booksellers, but expanding the market for books, at the expense of other kinds of purchase:

> It is not other bookshops that should be twitching at the growth of bargain bookshops but retailers that sell other traditional gift purchases – clothes, make up, sport and fashion accessories and so on.
>
> (Laura Bamford, *Bookseller*, 20 March 1992)

Similarly, not only does providing fiction in supermarkets give extra exposure to covers, familiarising the product and thus expanding the market in general, it also opens the door to the more sophisticated marketing and promotional tie-ups that are being used to sell all sorts of goods, not just books. For example, Julia MacRae made a deal with Safeway to produce their own brand children's books. High quality titles were supported by attractive stacking and header arrangements, backed up by a consumer competition (sponsored by Commodore computers) and advertised on Safeway milk cartons in the run up to Christmas 1992. Just as today the trend is for more marketing spend to be allocated to 'below the line' promotional arrangements rather than 'above the line' paid-for advertisements, books here are promoted as mainstream items rather than specialities. The resulting sales are new markets created, rather than stolen from anywhere else, and the general trend must surely benefit the whole business.

All these new locations meet real consumer need. The organisations which run school book fairs take their wares into the schools and often provide a financial incentive or 'kickback' for the school as a percentage of sales made – like any other party plan selling arrangement. When school funds are incredibly tight, particularly since the introduction of the local management of schools, this is a financial incentive that cannot be ignored.

Likewise, the sale of children's books through mail order and in supermarkets is effective because for busy mothers, with a couple of children in tow, that is the easiest way to buy.

I am told that whereas personnel managers (mostly arts graduates) are familiar with bookshop practice, finance directors are not. Would they be buying at all if not offered material through the post?

As proof of this need, the new locations work (Transworld estimated that 5 per cent of sales of Mary Wesley's *The Camomile Lawn* came through supermarkets). Supermarkets keep a close eye on sales levels to justify continued stocking; although retail margins on books are around twice as high as those on food, in general the stock turn is much lower. The selling of fiction in Sainsbury's supermarkets was brought in as an experiment from January – March 1992 and was so successful (sales are monitored in sales and profits per linear foot) that it was continued. Such supermarkets are hard nosed about results; any decision to continue stocking an item is based on sales-related feedback and nothing to do with enhancement of the range of products on offer. Sainsbury joined Tesco, Asda and Safeway in selling paperback fiction.

View 2: they provide unfair competition to bookshops
Many booksellers resent publishers selling to new locations and feel that trade should be directed to them as they stock in depth, rather than allowing other organisations to cream off the bestseller demand. They further complain that discount terms offered by publishers to non-traditional outlets, such as supermarkets or art and craft shops, are sometimes more favourable than the ones they receive themselves.

But publishers argue that the new markets have been there for booksellers to exploit too. Back in 1980 Sir Robert Lusty pointed out that books:

> should be on display and available wherever they apply: cookbooks in grocers; do-it-yourself books in hardware stores; books about wine in wine stores; fashion books in dress shops; health books in chemists. There is hardly a shop in the High Street in which books would be an irrelevance.

The Educational Publishers Council recently produced figures to show that 24 per cent of all books sold to schools are now sold direct. But selling in schools is an opportunity that bookshops could have developed further themselves. (Some do; I know one independent bookseller who runs stalls at Parent – Teacher evenings.) The editorial of the *Bookseller* concluded, after the 1992 Conference, that booksellers:

> should not be taken seriously if they call foul, solely on the basis of their own admirable commitment to books and the larger size and purchasing power of their competitors.

(15 May 1992)

It is several years since a BA conference spent most of the debating time discussing a motion critical of Walker Books for daring to sell books to Sainsbury's. But publisher bashing was back at the BA conference in May 1992, with President Malcolm Gibson castigating publishers for selling through book clubs, direct sales to non-traditional outlets and 'non-traditional organisations running book fairs in schools', a system he described as 'iniquitous'. But the market has moved on; all these outlets are thriving, and surely now *are* traditional.

Booksellers too must face the new trading conditions. Some independents have set up as specialists to reach particular markets, to stress the particular benefits such as depth of choice and product knowledge that they offer. For example, Fielders Educational Books of Wallington built a showroom and leafleted teachers about their service. But as director Richard Heth commented:

> Unless booksellers are prepared to work even harder than they currently are to attract customers, they are going to lose out to specialist suppliers and publishers.

> (*Bookseller*, 18 September 1992)

The struggle for new markets can be seen as part of a general trend: everything is tighter, for every kind of business. The Thatcherite spirit of self-help has been forced upon many firms by the effects of recession. Sutton led the way for libraries by opening the first library video lending service; running a profitable local history publishing programme; properly marketing their sales of withdrawn library stock (later supported by remainder and bargain books); renting umbrellas and running a coffee bar. Academic libraries are tying to make money by selling their services to the local business community; government departments are having to demonstrate more cost effectiveness.

In the same spirit, Reed now have a telesales unit that will supply any business interested in selling books – craft shops, cookery equipment stores, restaurants and so on. In addition to selling through retail outlets and direct mail initiatives, Reed's Rock 'n' Roll books are sold through the *New Musical Express* and *Vox* (both owned by Reed). They have for many years sold books as promotional items; for example, in return for test drives, or as both incentives and standard catalogue items in door-to-door and in-office sales. Random House are organising library days to tell librarians at first hand about their wares and offer them the chance to buy direct.

Publishers are also creating publishing arms to support these developments. For example, bargain bookshops at first sold remainder and imported stock. But for the past 12 years Bounty Books, part of Reed, have been producing stock especially for these outlets, as part of their integrated publishing programme. Other publishing groups (mainly Collins and Random House) are now starting to show interest in this area.

In the main, Bounty publish mass market hardbacks of popular books and sell them through outlets which the general public finds it convenient to buy through: motorway service areas and garage forecourts, supermarkets and bargain bookshops as well as the traditional book trade. Such titles are aimed at a specific market sector, and the product is therefore market led. Everything about it has to be right – size, price, look, illustrations – but for the right product the rewards can be enormous. Their bestselling omnibus edition of *The Silence of the Lambs* and *Red Dragon* has sold 320,000 copies (60,000 through the traditional book trade, 100,000 through BCA and 160,000 through bargain bookshops, service stations and other 'non-traditional' outlets).

In addition, new challenges to existing trade selling methods are emerging. After years of complaints from booksellers about the lacklustre choice of book token cards, and their continual promotion to only one sector of the possible market (adults buying for children), new ways of reaching the market have developed. Both Dillons and Waterstones have set up their own successful voucher schemes, harnessing their brand name to the undoubted benefits of the model provided by book tokens. (Dillons reported that in 1991 total voucher sales accounted for almost a sixth of the December turnover.) Now Inter-Book is offering a hardback delivery service, along the lines of Inter-Flora. You ring a number, quote the title required and the address, and for the price of the book, plus £4.99 for delivery (market research having shown that customers seeking the convenience of the service are relatively indifferent to price), and then leave it to them. A brilliant and convenient idea, and one can only hope that they have enough money invested in the service's future to ensure sufficient awareness.

2. The practicalities of selling through new locations
Many publishing houses now have a special sales manager looking at the new opportunities. For those who do not, the following should be considered:

- supermarket sales;
- garage forecourts;
- special sales through clubs (use someone else's or start your own);
- card decks;
- telemarketing;
- reps (with or without commission);
- identification of interest groups who are currently badly served and mailing them, eg publisher Godfrey Cave's direct marketing activities or bookseller Wyvern Crest targeting horse owners and lovers;
- parties;
- direct mail;

- cash and carry;
- van merchandising;
- door-to-door selling;
- 'premiums', ie sales promotion rewards for third parties;
- possibilities for cooperative selling to any of the above if you can't take them on yourself.

Before supplying new markets, the following consideration must be borne in mind for each location:

- how easy is it to service?
- how often will it need servicing?
- how high will wastage (theft) be? Books are portable and easily disguised (their relatively low cover price means that it is seldom worth the cost of electronically tagging them);
- stock on sale has to be product that is easily understood – there will be no staff around to explain;
- much less stock can usually be accommodated.

Period of time

Timing has always been an important sales opportunity in the book trade: diet and exercise books sell well in January; DIY and decorating titles in the spring; careers books for school leavers in May and June; beach reading is pushed in the summer. But of late, more specific, marketing-based initiatives that rely on timing can be seen. For example, the huge growth in the importance of literary prizes means that the marketing led activity surrounding them (timing of novel launch, promotional campaign, readiness for the reprint required if a title wins and so on) is dominated by the competition deadlines. Likewise, the fastest selling season of the year for the book business is the run up to Christmas (some estimate that 40 per cent of annual sales occur in this period), and all parts of the trade gear up to make their organisation function most efficiently then: distribution; promotion, public relations and so on.

Other specific publisher initiatives can be seen. Transworld showed great skill in launching the paperback of *Polo* right at the beginning of the month, which had the effect of offering booksellers an extra 30 days' credit.

Industry-wide promotions can seem less well planned. Why is it, several booksellers have asked, that the National Book Sale starts right after Christmas (usually 27 December), when customers visiting shops with book tokens can thus spend them on reduced, rather than full priced, stock? It would be much better to wait until February.

Profit

Profit is not the same thing as sales. A company may be selling its titles like hot cakes, but at the same time losing money. Similarly, if the margin between standard product costs and net sales value is insufficient, the company may not be making as much profit as is possible. As shown in the last chapter, there are lots of ways of calculating profit, and even more of monitoring it. I will stick to a few basic points.

1. Short- and long-term profit

Short-term profit needs to be compatible with long-term profit aims. Selling off the rights to your backlist may create much needed cash, and provide a short-term profit, but it may compromise the firm's long-term profitability. For example, after launching a new author and publishing his or her first few novels to little public acclaim, that author may subsequently become fashionable. Provided the rights to the backlist have been retained, copies can be brought out, dusted down (or if necessary reprinted), and the new interest capitalised upon.

For similar reasons, some firms sell rights to other companies with provision for review or 'clawback' at a later date. This provides a valuable insurance policy should the author decide to leave the original sponsoring publisher; the backlist cannot necessarily go too. For example, when Maeve Binchy decided to leave Random House, they clawed back the rights on her past paperbacks. The practice can also form the foundation of a successful new business. For example, one of the best-known examples of the 'clawback principle' was the launch of Mandarin Paperbacks by Reed, the first successful set-up of a paperback publisher in the UK for decades, and almost entirely based on a policy of reverting rights from Secker, Methuen and Heinemann titles. More recently, Reed negotiated the return of backlist rights for Wilbur Smith from Pan Macmillan to Mandarin.

2. Controlling costs

Controlling costs is perhaps easiest to do periodically, savagely and painfully: cut some new titles and live off the backlist; chop the marketing department budget; and, if the worst comes to the worst, make people redundant. This can be shortsighted.

Much more difficult, but in the long run much more beneficial, is the structured rethink, changing the culture of the company so that employees concentrate on making the best use of resources. If this is carried out, when trading conditions do improve, the company will have the products, marketing and service infrastructure, and determination, to develop demand fully.

3. Finding other sources

In addition to managing in-house finances better, there is the option of not bearing all the costs of publishing and promotion yourself. This has not traditionally been an area of great expertise in publishing:

> As an industry, we have been bad at developing other sources of income, such as taking advertising and encouraging sponsorship.
>
> (John Brown, *Viz*)

There are the large, industry-wide sponsors – Booker McConnell, Smarties, and more recently the *Daily Telegraph* (who provided £100,000 plus for Children's Book Week in 1992) and Dr David Cohen. But with the difficulties of the recession, individual publishers are increasingly turning to smaller levels of sponsorship or other means of financial contribution to help overheads:

> There is increasingly a need to find joint ventures or sponsorship or some added value, when you are scrabbling for every point of margin you can.
>
> (Harriet Spicer, Virago)

Some firm do this with straightforward sponsorship publishing. Quiller have been doing it for over ten years now. Their *French Entrée Guidebook* is sponsored by P & O, and *Enterprise on Canvas: British Industry through the Artist's Eye* by the CBI. A sponsor pays for, or contributes to, the costs of publishing, and in return receives prestige and promotion by being associated with a distinguished product. This is a profitable way to publish, and food and travel guides have long been produced in this way.

Others achieve similarly profitable results by working with sympathetic manufacturers in promotional or incentive deals. Reed are good at this: they organise cooperative ventures with charities and clubs; reciprocal arrangements with manufacturers to keep characters in the public eye. For example a Thomas the Tank Engine 45th Birthday was organised with the preserved steam railways and a big event held at the Didcot Railway Centre. The event attracted 25,000 visitors, who bought £14,000 worth of books and licensed products, and didn't really cost the publishers anything. Fireman Sam has been packaged with smoke alarms: Reed sold the manufacturers 60,000 books for a promotion. Spot's 10th Birthday was linked with Guide Dogs for the Blind, a benevolent approach that reflected well on all. Other firms are active too. 1993 is the centenary of Beatrix Potter's creation of Peter Rabbit, and major promotional link-ups are being run by Penguin, who now market Warne's list.

Looking to the future, there is more money to be made from linking products with publishers' copyright and licensing agreements. This started with product development (audio tapes of books already published) and merchandising (duvet covers, sweatshirts and soft toys) and is fast developing with more multi-media deals (CD/ROM and CDi [compact disk interactive]; computer games and simulations that develop the initial plot). Such spin-off deals are poised for rapid growth, and publishers need to establish tight controls over the use of materials now wanted for them. Some firms are ready to do this now. It is interesting that Microsoft own a significant part of Dorling Kindersley, and in April 1992 Penguin bought the whole share capital of Ventura Publishing, to expand their worldwide merchandising rights for Spot the Dog.

A trickier area is going to be who controls rights which perhaps did not actually exist at the time of the original contract. This is now preoccupying many publishers, particularly those involved in illustrated and reference publishing. Whereas 20 years ago author contracts mostly considered only other rights relating to audio-visual products, today it is important that new contracts cover future inventions, particularly in the area of electronic media. Some future legal wrangles can almost certainly be anticipated.

4. Approaching international markets

The export market has always been an integral part of British publishing activity. A general publisher in the UK expects to make around 35 per cent of total sales outside the home territory; a comparative figure for a US publisher would be around 2 per cent.

So, overseas deals are important. There are several ways in which arrangements for such sales can be made:

- overseas sale of the existing UK edition to specific markets;
- product creation specifically for a particular overseas market, either in this country or in the country in question, eg educational materials for developing countries;
- co-editions: making modifications to the basic product and then printing at the same time as the main edition, eg different language editions for illustrated titles which use the same pictures but different text (through black plate changes).

Achieving such overseas deals before going to print really does create economies of scale; Boxtree and Dorling Kindersley are just two firms which have reported the major part that such arrangements play in their overall profitability. Of course, the firm has to ensure pre-press that the product is absolutely right for the various external markets, and do the leg-work in sales, but the reward is a much longer print run, and hence competitive unit production costs. Illustrated publishers have been doing this for some time, with extensive print runs, all pre-sold overseas (runs of

100,000 of which 90,000 are pre-sold are not uncommon) and it perhaps explains why this particular area of publishing has survived the recession better than others.

But on the horizon in overseas markets are other changes of a more fundamental nature. The Henley Centre for Forecasting predicted at the start of this decade that: 'Almost everything influencing the success or failure of a business will be different by the year 2000.' There are several principal changes to watch out for.

The development of a free market and general regulatory framework in which the book trade operates, and from this the emergence of a pan-European publishing market

Since 1 January 1993 Britain has been part of the single market created by the EC. In theory, this means that all products must be available throughout the Community.

A growing Europeanism in publishing can certainly be detected already, a feeling that selling to Europe is not really exporting but developing the home market. Many firms still run their UK and European rep forces separately, but try to offer the same levels of service throughout the areas they serve.

Just as UK sales managers have their favourite stores, firms who analyse their European sales patterns find personalities emerging: the Copenhagen airport bookshop for business publishers; the Village Voice bookshop in Paris for literary publishers. The sale of European books has considerably increased in London with the expansion of a continental bookshop and a European Language Centre (both subsidiaries of a foreign language wholesaler, European Schoolbooks of Cheltenham). And the opening up of eastern Europe offers further opportunities – and risks.

In readiness to exploit the new opportunities of the single market, publishers seem to be well ahead of the game. Whether or not they have read them, their own titles on the single market of 1993 first appeared in 1988, and all business publishers are now well stocked on the subject. Planning for cross-European involvement can be seen in both formal industry association initiatives and networking between publishers and other interested parties. For example, the new head of the German publishers and booksellers association has suggested a collective European clearing point for the new single market, making use of the electronic transfer of data. The Euro-Business Publishing Network links European publishers, professional bodies and institutions for the exchange of ideas and manuscripts.

This European involvement is in sharp contrast with other industries. The Department of Trade and Industry's on-going research programme into business attitudes to the single market showed in 1991 that while 95 per cent of firms surveyed were aware of its imminence, only 43 per cent had taken any form of action to deal with the changes. A recent survey of management trends in British firms (*The Wealth Creators*, Andrew Kakabadse, Kogan Page, 1991) found that less than 33 per cent had formed any active policy for Europe, a further 30 per cent were opposed to forming any European strategy and the rest were non-committal.

American presence in European Markets

But the same opening up of markets in Europe creates an area of untested ambiguity about market rights, and British publishers may well start to look a little uneasily towards America.

A notable trend over recent years has been American investment in British publishing houses; there are few large firms today which are completely independent of US money. While most British companies still have near complete autonomy as to what they publish, this transatlantic linking means that market control can become global; the same edition of a book can be sold worldwide.

While US publishers have traditionally concentrated much more on the larger home market, their profitability there makes them financially well poised to expand. US print runs are significantly longer – an average paperback title may run to 14,000 in the UK; it would be more likely to touch 70,000 in the USA.

For those companies which do not have a transatlantic parent, and for the continued autonomy of those which do, the major worry in these difficult trading times is the arrival of the (sometimes earlier produced) US edition of a title in the European market, and the possibility that, following 1 January 1993, such editions may invade the already overcrowded UK market and Eire.

So far British publishers have been well placed to benefit from European integration. The flow of rights, on relevant titles, has been mainly one way, from Britain to the continent. There is also growing acceptance of English language text in southern Europe (northern European countries have always been good markets for British books). And American books do look unfamiliar in the European market. The US fondness for the use of foil, embossed lettering on covers and cheaper production standards, makes them easily identifiable. But one sales director assured me that the Americans are getting much better at exporting to Europe, and there is no doubt that increasing familiarity in the market-place will ultimately destroy the feeling of strangeness.

And cheaper American prices are a substantial determinant of interest. Warehouses in Europe, which are importing American titles now, mark them up to British levels, but one may speculate how long it will be before UK retailers try importing stock direct from the USA. This is an area yet to be tested, and I detect a degree of breath-holding.

There are other challenges to British publishing from overseas. Other nationalities have started publishing in English first; for example, German medical publishers such as Springer Verlag. This is a move no doubt fuelled by

> the realisation that in order to become a world force, publishing houses must move into the English-language market – the largest potential market in the world.
>
> (*European Book Publishing*, Datamonitor, 1992)

And in Australia, previously a distinct and important market for British books (the third largest English-speaking area), new legislation passed on 23 December 1991 has meant that the traditional right of British publishers to fix the time and price of Australian publication has been hedged around with restrictions on timing. A title must be available in Australia within 30 days of its original publication in *any other market*, or the territorial copyright is forfeited and any other legal edition may be sold (the principal opportunity being presented to the American publisher).

The progressive evolution of large transnational publishing companies

Achieved through merger, acquisition and internal growth, these can already be seen operating across a range of countries within and without Europe; for example, Groupe de la Cité and Masson in France, Elsevier in the Netherlands, Bertelsmann and Springer in Germany, and Reed and Pearson in the UK. All are seizing the opportunities for publishing on a global scale, and some are taking the move to merger even further: from 1 January 1993 Reed International and Elsevier united to form a new multi-billion pound business, Reed Elsevier.

Will British publishing end up being taken over by American publishing, and if so how long will it take? Or will British autonomy survive, supported by US funding? The degree to which British publishers are able to sell their wares overseas over the next few years is surely crucial.

Chapter 4

Industry Structure and Reputation

Letter to the *Bookseller*, 1 March 1991, from Mr AJ Webster, of the Book and Music Store, 11 Ship Street, Brecon, Powys, Wales:

> Sir, I have no doubt that the forthcoming London International Book Fair will be a time, among other things, for many publishers to revel in an orgy of self-satisfaction at the wonderful work they are doing taking the printed word to the populace.
>
> Last year, along with two colleagues, I attended my first LIBF with a view to promoting my new business to as many publishers unknown to us as possible. We visited as many stands as our day's visit would permit and, where we were not made to feel as though we were intruding on a private party or secret society meeting, left our business card and asked representatives to call.
>
> We returned to the wilds of Brecon feeling secure in the knowledge that soon our shelves would be bursting with books that our customers had been asking for. How naive we were! Not one company bothered to follow up our enquiries, and we are left to feel that the LIBF is no more than an old boys' reunion to offload as much petty cash as possible before the financial year end.
>
> One year later I wish I had a pound for every time that I have been told that the person at the other end of the telephone cannot help me because the computer has 'gone down' and a fiver for every rep who has not kept an appointment. LIBF? No thanks, I would rather buy stock to put on my shelves – that is assuming I can find anybody who wants to sell it to me.

This dispiriting letter highlights several important points about the UK book trade – how it works and how it is perceived by others within the same industry:

1. the impression that publishing is a closed shop, and publishers a self-appointed élite;

2. some genuine antipathy between publisher and bookseller;
3. increasing polarisation between large and small accounts;
4. regional polarisation: an industry dominated by the capital and centralised systems.

The decline of the calling representative has been a phenomenon of the
past few years; many publishers argue that it is uneconomic to send a rep
to small outlets if the order is then routed to a wholesaler (Macmillan took
this a stage further in August 1992 by effectively insisting that small
accounts use wholesalers). But the needs of Mr Webster could easily have
been met by effective use of replacement services such as teleselling. A year
on from the book fair, in April 1992, he reported that he was dealing
mainly through wholesalers.

All these factors have a bearing on the way the industry functions today,
and many highlight aspects that make the book trade 'different'. I plan to
start this chapter by looking at existing trade structures, and then examine
how issues of concern are dealt with in practice.

Trade organisations

Every now and again, someone will write to the *Bookseller* asking why it is
that the British book industry is represented by two, and not one, professional organisations: the Publishers Association (PA) and the Booksellers
Association (BA). Perhaps there is a natural clash of interests between the
suppliers and the supplied, which makes it impossible for the same
organisation to represent them both, but in other countries the situation is
different. In Germany, the Börsenverein represents both publishers and
booksellers and, what is more, is currently led by Gerhard Kurtze, a wholesaler.

The answers that invariably appear in the forthcoming weeks are pre-
dictable: each body meets the specific needs of its distinct membership;
neither could singly cover both. Yet to the outside world it is easy to
describe the book trade as both over-represented and introspective, perhaps in the same way that any other sharply defined group may be
depicted, such as barristers or sports stars.

Having looked into how other industries work, my conclusion is that it
is perhaps surprising that the book trade does not have *more*, not fewer,
representative organisations. For example, the grocery trade is served by a
great variety of different industrial and professional organisations. There
are those that look after the interests of different sizes of retailer (the British
Independent Grocers Association for the smaller stores, and similar
organisations for fishmongers, bakers and greengrocers; the Institute of

Grocery Distribution for the larger outlets). And there are those that span the retail sector and defend similar interests (the Federation of Small Businesses and the National Association of Shopkeepers for small outlets; the British Retail Consortium and the Multiple Retailers Association for the larger players). Similarly, the accountancy profession has three different professional representative bodies and lots of local associations, dining and lecture clubs.

The major changes in the book world that have taken place over the past few years have substantially altered the balance of power between the constituent members of the BA and the PA. But for the most part discussion has taken place within existing organisational structures rather than with the founding of new ones.

This changed balance of power within the book trade can be seen in the industry whenever a contentious issue arises (eg the launch of two new softback book clubs in 1991) and scorn is poured on the BA and the PA for 'failing to defend the interests of members'. In truth, neither organisation can claim that the interests of members are entirely compatible all the time.

This divergence of interests can be most easily observed within the membership of the Booksellers Association. Within the last ten years the market has been substantially affected by the arrival of major chains of booksellers, and the expansion of others: WHS (including Waterstones), Pentos, Books Etc, Blackwells, Heffers and so on. These firms have arrived at the cutting edge of the industry, absorbing or replacing the 28-year traditional lead provided by the Charter Group of professional booksellers, which has now disbanded (one of the final nails in the coffin was that only 20 people went along to the last AGM). The buying power of these chains is immense and has enabled them to if not dictate, at least greatly influence, terms from their suppliers: the publishers. Smaller members of the BA argue that this has been at the expense of the financial latitude allowed them by the same publishers.

Yet all belong to the same professional organisation, as indeed do Pentos, arch opponents of the NBA. Meanwhile the BA management, and the vast majority of its members, stress the need for the NBA to continue, as an essential support to the survival of independent booksellers. The then BA president, Malcolm Gibson, confirmed that while the BA was well pleased if:

> individual members are able to reach agreement for higher margins and extended credit periods with publishers as recommended by Arthur Young in their report *Book Retailing in the 1990s*, the BA is specifically

prevented by law by the Restrictive Practices Act from interfering in trading relationships between individual booksellers and their suppliers.
(letter to the *Bookseller* 20 September 1991)

Independent bookshop owners regard this as the BA bucking responsibility for the majority of members; they think that such a restriction:

does not mean that such a defence is either illegal or impractical.
(Laurence Cohen and Mary Ashenden, letter to the *Bookseller* replying to Mr Gibson, 11 October 1991)

Both they, and others, have suggested that a group of independent book-sellers, who comprise 80 per cent of the membership of the BA, should join together to lobby for terms close to those granted to the chains and explore cooperative buying and negotiating arrangements. Other independent booksellers, such as Matthew Huntley of P & G Wells in Winchester, have argued that a similar grouping of independents should be stressing the advantages that smaller shops have to offer: service, choice, atmosphere and customer orientated individual care. In other industries such arrangements do work.

Again, a comparison with the grocery trade is relevant and interesting: 25 years ago there were 100,000 independent grocers in the UK, some with multiple outlets such as Sainsbury's and Asda. Today there are only around 40,000 independents and the market is dominated by five leading multiples. But in the grocery business the independents cannot look to the government for practical help, such as the restrictive practice of resale price maintenance in the book trade; their solution has been self-help. The British Independent Grocers Association serves its members as a political watch-dog and lobbier; offers on-going public relations on the value of the independent retailer and provides members with an advisory service, as well as other practical benefits such as low insurance rates. For similar reasons, many smaller retailers join cooperative buying arrangements, whether retailer or wholesaler owned, which ensure that they gain better prices than they would by buying individually (eg through organisations like Spar, Maceys, VG, Nisa and Londis). Wherever they buy their stock, the Association's secretary Alan Taylor concluded that those independents who are surviving best are those who accept that 'life is not fair'; that different discounts are available to the multiples – and then get on with competing with them, often head on. Such stores can promote the local and convenient service that they offer as well as their low prices, which are frequently lower than the multiples who have shareholders to satisfy and thus must reflect dividends in their store prices.

The small independent BA members have often suggested that their needs are forgotten. Although they may suggest grouping to act in defence of their joint interests, when most are owner-managers, sparing the time would be difficult; it is a function that they feel should be handled by their professional organisation. Complaints that the BA is dominated by the larger chains are refuted by Mr Gibson:

> Blackwells, Pentos, WH Smith and Waterstones have 619 shops in a BA membership of 3204, 19.3 per cent. Five of the 25 members of the BA Council come from these firms.
>
> (letter to the *Bookseller*, 20 September 1991)

But this is muddling specific geographical location with overall financial grouping. Individual branches of Waterstones and Dillons do their buying autonomously, but the discounts they receive are scaled to the clout of the chain as a whole (and there are many centrally agreed promotions). WHS buy centrally, have stock delivered to their warehouse in Swindon and then distribute from there.

Similarly, to an observer from any other industry it would seem obvious that larger accounts receive larger discounts. Here again the 'differentness' of books crops up. Because books are overlaid with the wide-reaching benefits (the importance of access to information; the value of literacy; the necessity of having available a wide variety of literature and so on), economic reality is laid aside in pursuit of the greater good. This is the morality of the argument for maintaining the funding of local libraries, applied to the economics of the high street.

At the same time the BA has centralised administration into an organisation that is able to respond to changes more quickly, and reduced the size of an unwieldy council and the power of local branches. Regional members, meanwhile, argue that the BA is already over-centralised.

The Net Book Agreement (NBA)

These problems are crystallised in difficulties over the Net Book Agreement. It is worth examining the issues involved in further detail as they say a lot about differences between the publishing industry and the rest of the world, notably:

1. public concern to discuss and express ways in which the industry may progress;
2. private evasion of the NBA and deal making;
3. endless discussion and genuine uncertainty about what would happen should the terms of business be changed.

81

The BA sees the NBA as the cornerstone of its support for the independent bookseller. Yet this agreement is one between publishers, and not booksellers, and the PA can only advocate that agreement as long as its membership agrees.

It is important to remember that the PA is a representative organisation, not an independent one. The BA would like the PA to put forward the morality of the argument for keeping the NBA and force its membership to toe the line; in practice the PA is empowered to represent only what its members want. In any case, the last full referendum on the NBA by the PA was in 1988, before the most recent arguments for its scrapping were aired. (Then 70 per cent of responding members declared themselves in favour of the agreement.) A more recent survey in 1991, by Coopers and Lybrand, showed that 99 per cent of publishers believe that it is on its way out. And in July 1992 the European Commission outlawed the operation of the NBA across EC trade frontiers, as an infringement of Community competition rules, by restricting trade between member states (although the operation of the NBA in the domestic markets is unaffected).

And on the NBA, PA membership, in private at least, seems to be divided. Smaller publishers argue that loss of the NBA would substantially increase the buying power of the big bookselling chains to secure even greater discounts, and hence dramatically reduce their own margins. They look to the PA for support. Larger publishers meanwhile cannot, or will not, ignore the enormous buying powers of the chains and are happy to negotiate from positions of strength, despite their usually public support for the NBA.

The rules are broken all the time. The book club Quality Paperbacks Direct (QPD)'s initial stock was made available without notice to the trade, and before all editions had been available in bookshops for the required six months. International airports can sell trade editions long before they are available in UK shops. Dillons have been accused of encouraging abuses of the library licence system, in contravention of the NBA, by extending the 10 per cent discount on net books to university departments, school and staff purchases, but other retailers, both large and small, have in the past not been guiltless in this respect.

Terry Maher of Pentos has complained of double standards; different opinions have been expressed to him in public and private by key figures in the book trade. And there certainly seem to be a number of publishers who cheer the agreement 'from the top of the fence'. Yet would reducing the PA to an industry police force deny the industry's dynamism, impede good ideas? Are rules there to be broken? It makes the PA Chief Executive's task all the more difficult. As Clive Bradley recently commented, running a membership organisation is 'exceptionally difficult'.

Your resources are tiny in proportion to the problems you have to deal with. The normal rules of management go out of the window. Members do not join an association to do what they are told; instead, they all expect you to do what they tell you, and if that happens to conflict with what another member thinks, then that's your problem.

(*Publishing Research Quarterly*, January 1993)

Reasons for, and consequences of, scrapping the NBA

Why are people trying to change it? Motives are variously ascribed.

1. To expand the market for books, using price as an element of the marketing mix; to encourage more people into bookshops (Terry Maher).
2. To pursue market freedom and allow competition; as an extension of Thatcherite self-help values and the competition policy provision of the Treaty of Rome (the Institute of Economic Affairs, a right-wing think tank; a variety of MPs and opinion shapers; most of the media who report the issue).
3. To further the interests of specific businesses; to gain market share from competitors and push up the company's share value (the detractors of Terry Maher). 'It's all about market share, sales and profits, not principle,' said Julian Blackwell.

Possible results of the loss of the agreement

Pentos argue that the market for books would expand; discounts would attract more people into bookshops; more new and existing book buyers would be spending more. What is certainly true is that in the months after price protection was withdrawn there would be a determined struggle by WH Smith, including Waterstones, to protect their own market share.

It is probably true that a few smaller independent firms – both booksellers and publishers – might well go out of business, but equally those with strong local traditions of service or market specialisations would most likely continue to thrive, benefiting from the higher profile of their product and the new markets. Small quality publishing houses would probably be less prepared to take risks with adventurous publishing decisions, backing new authors.

Among both booksellers and publishers there would almost certainly be concentrations of power: the big would become bigger and the small would be proportionately disadvantaged. This has already happened in markets where resale price maintenance has been abolished, such as Australia; the number of outlets is constant, but they are concentrated in fewer hands. In the UK wine trade (no *rpm*) large outlets are able to block distribution from wholesalers to smaller shops which try to undercut them, and to do this on the grounds of 'unfair competition'. Smaller publishers are already complaining of huge discounts (52.5 per cent plus), extended credit and difficulty in getting to see buyers in the larger chain owned bookshops. (For example, in 1989 WH Smith stopped reps visiting most of their branches; calls from the reps of major paperback houses were phased out in July 1991. Buying decisions are based on information derived from central EPOS statistics.)

After the initial rush of discounting, few genuine discounts would probably survive. Many books would be announced at artificially high prices in the first place to enable them to be discounted. For example, resale price maintenance was abolished 20 years ago in Australia, but discounting is not widespread; it is usually restricted only to bestsellers. Similarly, in Belgium, out of 60,000 titles available, only around 2000 are discounted, and on these cover prices have been raised to allow for lost margins. There are charges for special services (eg ordering) and fewer books are produced. In America lower margins have meant that customer service is, in many cases, now minimal:

> Price maintenance is dead: the result is mass production for a mass market, and a minimum of service. If you want something out of the ordinary, you go and hunt for it, and the best of American luck.

(Cynthia Reavell, Martello Bookshop in Rye, *Bookseller*, 3 January 1992)

To make up for the margin lost on bestsellers, a wider variety of other books would probably be marked up, as is already the case with non-net educational and academic texts. In the long term this would most likely result in generally higher prices and fewer books produced. In other words, the main benefit expressed to the market by those committed to abolishing the NBA, ie lower prices, would almost certainly not apply, and the variety of titles on offer, especially in general fiction, would be reduced. In Australia it is worth noting that there have been three government enquiries into the high price of books since 1972.

Smaller bookshops would probably be forced to rely more on wholesalers and so their range of stock would be reduced. The returns rate would probably go up – in the US it averages 25 – 30 per cent for bestselling fiction. The price war in the music business has not led to market growth or lower prices but the emergence of WH Smith as the leading player.

How the debate has progressed

This debate has become very personal, but clear hatred ('the rapaciousness of particular chain booksellers and the craven attitude of publishers to their demands') has not produced effective opposition. One could argue that such attitudes have served only to spur on Terry Maher; after all, what has he got to lose?

The BA employed a public relations agency to put forward arguments for the retention of the NBA. Arguably, an issue they felt so strongly about should have been handled in-house; certainly the resulting column inches on keeping the agreement were slim. News journalists have proved reluctant to master the benefits of retaining the NBA, and in any case much prefer to depict a 'mould breaker' taking on the system, and publishing as an inefficient and old-fashioned communication medium.

Should the publishing industry be congratulated on having maintained its 'different' status for so long? Today there is only one other type of product to benefit from legally binding retail price maintenance: some pharmaceutical medicines. The abolition of *rpm* in the 1960s on most other goods led to the opening of, for example, the discount furniture and carpet warehouses with their continual sales that we see today.

> I have always believed that the original upholding of the NBA owed as much to the supremely effective connections of the publishing industry in the body politic as to the pure quality of the arguments deployed.
>
> (Michael Sissons, literary agent)

Ultimately though, I suspect that over-concentration on the benefits of keeping or scrapping the NBA largely misses the point: expanding or contracting the market for books is not just a function of the NBA; indeed, many of the possible future scenarios described by those who want to keep it are already taking place. I know that the BA was formed in 1895 with the express purpose of ending 'underselling' (or discounting), but perhaps it is time to widen the issue, to look less at the mechanics of business and more at the opportunities. Those who discount report increases in profits, but does this bear witness to the effectiveness of promotion in general, to a market unused to it, or the efficacy of price cutting in particular?

Over the last ten years the NBA has not prevented the huge growth of the chains (50 per cent of the retail market is now in the hands of four chains), the increasing polarisation of the business, the dramatic development of non-retail sales. Publishers do not produce a huge selection of titles in the interests of a diverse trade but in the expectation of making money. Booksellers stock them in the hope of meeting demand, not of producing a classification system that competes with their local library. And the massive increases in high street rents of the early to mid 1980s, and in some areas the Uniform Business Rate, will have much bigger effects on high-stock, low-turnover trades such as books, toys and ironmongery than the removal of retail price maintenance.

Concentration on price maintenance fails to take into account whether people buy books at all, but focuses instead on people buying one book in preference to another, or in one place rather than another. We should be seeking to expand the market in real terms, not steal market share. As Gordon Graham put it in an interview in the *Bookseller*, 13 July 1990:

> Books are still different, but they are also different from what they were. Today the question is whether we are using price maintenance optimally in a market-place where the most serious competition is not between publisher and publisher or between bookseller and bookseller, but between books and other commodities.

A compromise position

In his address to the BA conference in May 1991 Paul Scherer, President of the PA, mentioned the PA's recent statement:

> underlining the flexible nature of the agreement, which is such that if publishers wish to publish some, or all, general trade books non-net, then they are at liberty to do so.

In other words, publishers are free to use the non-net category, traditionally reserved for low discount, bulk sale items such as educational texts, for general trade books. In this way Cassell in 1991 de-netted their dictionary range while asserting the continued value of the NBA:

> The NBA should stay. It already allows sufficient flexibility for price promotion in the trade, as our initiative demonstrates.
>
> (Philip Sturrock, Chairman, quoted in the *Bookseller*, 3 May 1991)

Price *is* important in the marketing of books today, as the growth of own brand publishing in supermarkets, the expansion of book clubs and remainder bookshops have shown, and there is surely room for some flexibility – perhaps the support of stable rather than fixed prices.

> my view is that the book world recognises that price can be as powerful a weapon as it is in any other business.
>
> (Matthew Evans, *Independent on Sunday*, 24 March 1991)

Should we consider Gordon Graham's idea for a new category of pricing for some books based on recommended retail price (RRP), which could be discounted to attract the public into shops, or some flexibility to incorporate promotional items in cover price to add value as suggested by Andrew Welham of Penguin? Is it always true that what a trade with as many products as the book industry needs is constant pricing, or should we more realistically agree that:

> once in a while a little discounting might inject some vigour into the market?
>
> (Clare Somerville, Marketing Director of Octopus quoted in an interview in the *Bookseller*, 13 March 1992)

Certainly, the longer this debate goes on, the more damaging to the health of the book it becomes. Already the most likely long-term outcome of the NBA debate is that the general public will think books are too expensive; conversations at the bookshop point of sale confirm that this is happening already – a tragedy. Piles of discounted books in high street stores make them all look like remainder merchants. We need to build on the public's inbred perception of books as high value items, a perception that has outlasted the scrapping of retail price maintenance in Australia (see page 63).

Industry cooperation

The image persists of publishing as a small world: 'people from Hampstead publishing books by and for people from Hampstead'.

> 'I have seldom met a business where the units seem to be smaller and where the gossip and the politics appear to be greater than in the publishing business ... Openness doesn't seem to be a characteristic of your business.'
>
> (Sir John Harvey-Jones, speech at LIBF, April 1991)

Publishers attend each other's parties in the Groucho; take turns to pursue what Julian Rivers called the 'W circuit for new books' (warm white wine and Wogan) and contribute to literary life in London. Many firms have now left what was the traditional heart of publishing, Bedford Square, and established themselves in other civilised cities – Oxford, Cambridge, Edinburgh, Bristol and Cheltenham – as the range of local services, such as training and design, that have grown with them in these new localities, shows. Networking and mutual support are much in evidence (eg the shadowing and job finding schemes set up by the PA and BA; Women in Publishing mentoring and training schemes).

Industry cooperation is essential to some degree. It is a function of the number of titles in print, and their wide availability in all outlets through ordering if not stocking. It is none the less remarkable. Try ordering a Country Casuals dress from Selfridges if they do not currently stock it, or getting your local corner shop to stock your favourite brand of biscuits without promising to take the whole 'outer' of 48 packets should no one else in the neighbourhood like them.

Much industry cooperation takes place at trade organisation level. For example, the PA and the BA get together to investigate particular areas of concern such as distribution; they are co-sponsors, with the British Library and the Library Association, of Book Industry Communications (BIC), a new company set up in 1991 to oversee book trade standards. In 1966 WH Smith funded standardisation through the establishment of an ISBN system (devised by a committee of Smiths, the PA's Distribution and Methods Committee and other experts). Bar codes emerged in the same way. In other areas cooperation has been taken further, as in the amalgamation of the Booksellers Association trade exhibition and the London International Book Fair, it having become clear that there simply was not enough custom to run two major trade fairs in the UK every year. (The BA was compensated for the loss of revenue.)

The trouble is that industry cooperation can be slow, particularly if it is hampered by naked commercial interests. Just as politicians are often accused of playing for time when they commission enquiries about particular problems, the same is often true of industry working parties.

Other traditional industry groupings are breaking down or weakening. As already mentioned, the Charter Group of Booksellers no longer exists, and after years of extremely active involvement in the Educational Publishers Council under Alan Hill and Hamish MacGibbon, Heinemann Educational Books can no longer participate as Reed, which now owns it, does not now belong to the PA.

But new alliances are being forged, and taking place in 'non-traditional' settings. Industry members who do continue to give freely of their time are from a wider variety of firms: wholesalers, publishers and booksellers, size and dynamism being better indicators of values in common than specific market-place origin. For example, Book Marketing Ltd has hosted some interesting groupings of speakers from across the industry, and the same names are appearing at the Society of Authors, the Society of Young Publishers, and in interviews with *Marketing Week*, *The Economist* and the quality papers as well as under the auspices of the PA and the BA.

And in 1991 even the fiercely competitive wholesaling world was demonstrating cooperation, when three of the largest firms, Barnicoats, Heathcote and Bertrams issued a joint press release saying that they would adopt the Book Industry Communications standard for electronic ordering and order confirmation, for although 'we are competitors in book supply, we do not wish to compete in supply of bookshop computer systems'.

How far we should try to profit further from what would seem to be an endemic belief in the value, if not the practicalities, of industry coopera-tion, I will look at next. Are generic promotions desirable – or even possible?

Generic promotions

If publishing is an industry with a good degree of cooperation between its main players, and a pressing need, as Frank Delaney put it, to 'widen the constituency for books', why doesn't this take the form of extensive generic advertising? Could the whole industry unite behind slogans like 'read a book, it's great' or 'go to work on a book'?

The arguments for generic advertising are well rehearsed in the trade, and each time they are aired they are greeted with the same cynicism or downright hostility. But the issue is not dead. Writing in the summer 1991 edition of *Bookselling News* Malcolm Gibson suggested that 'generic mar-keting is essential if we are to expand the market for books'.

He proposed that a small levy should be added to the price of each book sold, and the profits – perhaps as much as £20 million a year – used to fund a generic campaign. Others felt that the money would be put to more effect in increasing the market for books by attacking illiteracy, as:

> Books are so various in their natures, and the needs and motivations of readers as manifold, that a simple appeal to 'go out and buy a book' – however skilfully expressed – is unlikely to address the hearts of more than a very small proportion of the reading public.
>
> (Daniel Easterman, letter to the *Bookseller*, 27 September 1991)

But who would coordinate this effort? Therein lies the rub. BA Marketing initiatives have frequently hit difficulties owing to publishers' 'severe bud-get restraints in the present economic climate'. Generic marketing is the kind of work that the Book Marketing Council, then part of the PA, did in the early 1980s with their Best of British campaigns, but which was floated off because of the Association's own budgetary constraints.

Gibson said his initiative should be coordinated by an 'independent trade-driven marketing agency'. Easterman thought an equally vague 'association of publishers, booksellers, authors and others ought to be put together for the purpose of raising and disbursing funds for just such a series of campaigns'. Others have suggested that perhaps Book Tokens could coordinate such an effort. Barry Winklemann of HarperCollins pledged £200,000 from Collins for a £2 million TV advertising campaign for books, but no one else came forward to join him.

89

Nevertheless, some have tried. The trouble is that you then get committee decisions.

- The joint advertisement by booksellers and publishers for children's books that appeared in the *Independent on Sunday* in April 1992 was a remarkable feat of organisation, with the Children's Book Foundation acting as bankers. The ad served the wider aim of encouraging newspapers to provide more editorial space for children's book reviews, drawing its inspiration from the North American market, and the initial experiment has been repeated twice since then. But the ad had no clear message. It included 17 different addresses. There was an instruction, in brackets, '(mail order is available)', but no coupon. Very different from the clear QPD ad two pages earlier 'start with any 5 from only 50p each' and a coupon that was easy to fill out.
- In Australia a second generic book campaign in a decade was launched on 1 December 1991 with the slogan: 'Life's better with a book.' The campaign was coordinated by the Australian Publishers Association but largely paid for from the royalties of an existing trademark slogan, previously loaned out. The campaign benefited from community service advertising slots on television.

Probably the best way of promoting generically is through specific brand advertising which, whether the advertisers like it or not, has a knock-on effect for other industry members. This is the way that generic ads have worked in other industries; for example, the creation of new markets through the promotion of specific branded goods, such as fabric conditioner and share ownership. For instance, the following are all, in effect, generic promotions for books:

- Books clubs, launched by individual companies. John Roberts, editorial and sales director of BCA, says that book clubs such as QPD are 'introducing a new group of young, educated people to regular book buying, book awareness' (*Bookseller*, 11 October 1991), providing extra promotion for the titles included in the selection and a boost to the whole industry. Wyvern Crest claim that for every 100,000 books they sell through the mail, a further 60,000 are sold through bookshops. Michael Joseph found that the inclusion of a Dick Francis title in a book club selection always led to extra bookshop sales: from those who wanted the book but not the club commitment.
- Other specific promotional deals arranged between individual publishers and distributors. For example, selling books through supermarkets and advertising books as promotional items on the back of cereal packets

reaches millions of literate people, and hence potential book buyers, who might not go into bookshops.

- There is also the occasional marketing gem in this area. In the past it proved difficult to get publishing company hierarchies to agree to the marketing of their books as products in competition with other products. For example, there were angry scenes in one house over a Christmas ad in the early 1980s headlined 'There are some gifts Santa wants to keep for himself', with a picture of a selection from the Christmas list. The sales director insisted that the word 'gifts' be replaced by 'books', thereby considerably weakening the message.

  Thankfully, this attitude is changing as evinced by the promotional campaign mounted by Puffin in the summer of 1992 which focused on their brand with both style and truth. The picture showed a measuring gauge being fitted to a child's foot, with the caption, 'Puffin can do the same for your child's mind'.

- Finally, there is certainly a role for a lobbying group to act on behalf of books as Mr Gibson suggested. But harnessing 'popular culture', as he advocated, need not cost a fortune. What is needed is an opportunities spotter, such as used by the major charities, to see that books are included as often as possible, anywhere the public will see them. For example, could the director of *Coronation Street* be asked to ensure that a certain character is often shown reading; does Shula Archer read romantic fiction or the Booker shortlist? Could more widespread coverage for juicy bookish headlines be achieved, such as Madonna's little noted: 'Everyone thinks I'm a nymphomaniac, but I'd rather read a book.' Specialist agencies place branded goods in films and commercial television series. Is there a role for a publishing industry body to do that?

That is positively the final mention for the possible role of an 'industry body' in this area. Generic advertising is probably best left to individual firms to organise. It does not work collectively, not because books are too diverse, but because vested interests are too competitive.

Trade publications

Finally, a word on trade publications. The main thing to note is the immense domination of J Whitaker & Sons Ltd, which also runs a great variety of other publishing services, including an enormous database, the basis for *British Books in Print*, now available in a variety of different formats.

Like the proprietors of most newspapers, the Whitaker family put forward a strong point of view. One could certainly argue that the most consistent voice on the benefits of maintaining the NBA has been advanced by them over the past ten years.

Terry Maher was allowed to use the pages of the *Bookseller* to explain his views, but not before the anti-abolition arguments had been voiced in the earlier news pages (issue of 17 February 1989). The Consumers Association report into the NBA was reported as basically pro, and it was left to Richard Charkin to point out in a letter the following week (which, to be fair, was printed) that the news item had left out the report's conclusion that:

> One clear message is that there is a case for more widespread non-netting of books (for example, bestsellers), where greater price competition would be an unambiguous improvement of the bookbuyer's lot ... this much-needed change of policy, which can still be operated within the framework of the NBA ...

Chapter 5

External Attitudes: What the World Outside the Book Trade Thinks of Books

This chapter will take a look at attitudes towards books from those outside the industry. Do they see books as 'different', and if so, why?

For both publishers and booksellers there are certainly difficulties in selling a product that is in the main both intellectual and demanding, and it is worth analysing these factors in greater detail.

1. The requirement of literacy

Publishers are producing a product that requires, with few exceptions, the ability to read:

> No book attains any purpose unless it is read.
> (Sir Robert Lusty, paper given to the Library Discussion Group of the Royal Institution, reproduced in the *Bookseller*, 21 June 1980)

Yet is reading going out of fashion? Bemoaning the standards of literacy in our schools is a favourite on 'news light' days: x per cent of our under seven-year-olds cannot read fluently; x per cent of our school leavers cannot spell and do not know what a verb is. And if publishers worry about falling standards of literacy among today's young people eroding their margins, there is the added concern for fashions in education that continue to exert a wholly negative effect on the book trade.

The much publicised 'purifying' of children's libraries by removing the works of Enid Blyton *et al* in the 1970s has left a damaging legacy: lack of confidence among sectors of the population who do not buy many books. How many potential book buyers, in particular those choosing presents, decide not to buy a book on the off-chance of getting it wrong, and so revealing their ignorance?

2. Government protection and the public interest

> if there is nothing to differentiate a book from a bar of soap, or the book
> market from the car market, then why are they not taxed in the same way?
>
> (Peter Bagnall of Blackwells, *Bookseller*, 7 June 1991)

Books are treated as a different kind of merchandise by the government.

First, there is no VAT on books, and the same applies to newspapers and other educational products. But the list of exemptions is slim: usually basic commodities/services with a strong public benefit. Children's clothes, most food, transport, drugs and medicines and aids for handicapped people all benefit, but theatre tickets, educational videos, computer software and museum entrance (substantially down since charges were introduced, incidentally) do not. And this has been the position for some time: books and journals have been exempted from taxation in this country for over 130 years, in the common belief that an impost on knowledge was an act against the public good – a measure that, as Gladstone told the Commons in 1860, had 'long stood in evil odour in this House'. When purchase tax was introduced at the beginning of the Second World War, books were exempted, and the exemption continued when in 1973 the purchase tax system was replaced by VAT.

The same goes in much of Europe; the zero rate of purchase tax on books looks set to remain in force following the recent publication of the EC's revised draft directive on VAT on books and other 'socially important items' (25 May 1990). Where VAT is charged, it is often at a lower rate than that generally prevailing (eg Germany charges a special 7 per cent on books, the general rate being 14 per cent).

Second, the courts have continued to uphold retail price maintenance (it remains to be seen what change the recent European Court ruling will bring). Although a body of opinion among Conservative MPs seemed to be gathering against the agreement, in the event the NBA's abolition was not included in the last Conservative Manifesto, and thus is not officially part of the current government's policy.

Third, the government accounts for a large chunk of publishers' sales – for example, to schools and libraries – and so has a great ability to influence the profitability of publishing. There is, perhaps, an irony in governments declaring the public interest of books and then cutting back the amount of money available.

> The Government believes that book loans should be free. The aim of the free public library service is to provide individuals with access to literature and information which will enable them to play their part in the country's cultural, political and economic affairs.

(Spokesman for the Department of National Heritage to Graham Lord, *Daily Telegraph*, 24 January 1993)

But controls on local government spending, the demands of installing the National Curriculum and centrally awarded teachers' pay increases have placed severe strain on schools' finances. Most have had to cut back the amount they can allocate from their budget to the purchase of books.

And we all accept that we should pay to access other potentially 'educational' media such as films, or our licence fee for the BBC.

The importance of the governmental attitude towards books was discussed during a session on the book trade's responsibilities entitled 'Books – in the public interest?' at the BA conference in May 1991. Lamenting cuts in school spending and library budgets, Paula Kahn of Longman concluded:

> We cannot have a market that will grow and develop until government attitudes to creating readers change fundamentally.

The Arts Minister, Tim Renton, accused the other panel members of passing the parcel of responsibility for people not buying books on to the government, but confirmed the original assumption by suggesting some sort of monitoring body to keep an eye on whether only those authors who have received the largest advances have their books looked after. In other words, he was separating publishing from the economics of ordinary business into a public service for the dissemination of information and education.

At the same time, the close association of books with government practice, as 'official products', may perhaps have a negative effect on sales:

> What we are trying to do is get away from the idea that books are like medicine: good for you but not particularly pleasant.
>
> (Richard Charkin, managing director of Reed Consumer Publishing)

The majority of the buying public do not appreciate the fine detail of arguments for and against price setting or purchase taxes, but there is a natural assumption that intervention is bad for the consumer. Would less citing of the public interest mean less concentration on the issues of accessibility and price, to the long-term benefit of the trade? Is it really true that:

> resale price maintenance and the orderly marketing of books are fundamentally a matter of public interest, not merely a matter of economic concern to booksellers and publishers.
>
> (Michael Zifcak)

Or does the very fact of government involvement dull a product by association, perhaps in the same way as the disestablished Church in the USA is said to be growing far faster than the established Church of England. And the creation of special governmental categories of merchandise allows through some spectacularly inappropriate examples – David Sullivan's soft porn magazines too are free from VAT.

3. The amount of consumer involvement required before purchasing a book, compared with other products

Whether or not they still admit to it, it is common for those in the book trade slightly to resent large, mass-market, chain stores talking about 'products', 'brand names' and 'premium versions' when what they are really talking about are different types of book. But a book is a product with a price, just like a packet of fish fingers. Nevertheless, differences between buying the former and the latter emerge almost immediately.

A book is not a life essential, or is not marketed as such

The parent in a supermarket, whose children love fish fingers, is confronted with a relatively simple yes/no decision on whether or not to buy some. This is followed by a 'which one?' decision (how much do they cost; do I want mostly breadcrumbs or mostly fish inside; what special offer is on the pack; have the children already picked up the packet with the Mickey Mouse cartoon on it?). The alternative is a 'what instead?' decision (fish cakes, sausages or pizza?). But answering one of the two questions is imperative as they must eat something, and the parent's very presence in the shop implies need.

No other product requires such commitment from the purchaser at such a low purchase price

One large (36) pack of fish fingers costs about the same as a paperback book, but whereas fish fingers are available in shops selling other forms of merchandise, books are mostly sold only in shops selling just other books. Our local supermarket stocks three brands of fish fingers; the decision to buy cannot take that long. But the sheer number in which books are available, immensely complicates the decision-making process.

For example, on a Saturday morning I can decide to spend £25 on myself. The decision to buy a new shirt is relatively simple: does the shop have my size, a colour I think suits me and in a material I can machine-wash? This may reduce the decision to a straight choice between two or three items, all of which I can try on before I make my choice. The process is the same for a new handbag or a pair of shoes.

If, on the other hand, I decide to spend the money on books, the selection process will almost certainly take longer. Not only do I, in most cases, have to leave a department store where all the other items are available, and head for a specialist book store, but the variety on offer is immense. Should I decide to buy one high-priced hardback, I need make only one decision, but if I decide to spend the money on paperbacks, it could be multiplied up to five times. The book buyer must confront the complexities of making a decision every time he buys (am I likely to enjoy this book; shall I read a few paragraphs to establish this; what is the contents list; have I read a book by this author before; have I even heard of him or her?). And that is assuming that he or she feels comfortable making these decisions in the place of sale.

Whether through nature or nurture, there is a perceived and qualitative difference between deciding to buy a book and deciding to buy something else. This is a difference that book-buying adults may dismiss, and that publishers may try to change, but which still persists.

4. Higher expectations that neglect commercial realities

Few industries straddle the opposing interests of art and business as uncomfortably as book publishing.

(*The Economist*, 7 April 1990)

No other category of merchandise gets all the free space allocated to books through reviews and features. The *TLS* used to lose £100,000 a year. Is this 'quite a modest sum by the standards of serious weekly journalism' and the price to be paid for flagship quality (Quentin Oates, *Bookseller*, 9 November 1991), or something the paper's owner must seek to change? Jeremy Treglown's subsequent departure made it look as if harsher realities were to prevail.

The president of the Library Association may lament (November 1990) that:

scholarly publication is coming more and more into the hands of firms whose main or sole concern is profit rather than the dissemination of scholarship

but this does not take account of the many reasons other than dissemination of scholarship that mean people want to be published. Today, getting a job, gaining security of tenure and getting promotion all seem to depend on a 'publications' section at the end of a scholar's CV. To that end, although publication in a refereed publication is preferable, many academics are satisfied to see a paper divided into smaller sections and published in a variety of commercial journals; it gives them more references to quote. And surely the competition to be published is one of the hurdles that keeps the quality of papers submitted high.

Libraries have long emphasised the access they offer to information rather than, in terms of on-line searches and the time of trained archivists, what it actually costs to retrieve it. This attitude has trickled towards the publishing world and, in the long term, is probably not helpful.

The general public have come to assume that enthusiastic information provision and profit are somehow incompatible when dealing with books. Jane Cholmeley of the Silver Moon Women's Bookshop told me that she is often asked if theirs is a non-profit making organisation: somehow it is assumed that service provision and the depth of commitment from an all-female staff imply that the work is being done for love rather than money. As Roisin Conroy of the Attic Press (Ireland's feminist press) commented: 'We are non-profit taking, not non-profit making.'

5. The application of different standards of morality to the book trade in comparison with other industries

Is what publishers produce and booksellers stock simply their own business, or does their effect on the 'public interest' award them higher responsibilities? Should market forces be the only guide to what publishers are producing, or should they be using their profits to subsidise less highly valued information, to lead the market?

In advocating the widespread availability of books, publishers are apt to claim that books are nothing different, and are capable of being sold anywhere the buying public would like to find them:

> If books apply to life and the living of it, they must accept the roughness and toughness of the market-place. There is nothing sacrosanct about the printed word or the book.
>
> (Sir Robert Lusty, ibid)

Similarly, were WH Smith stocking anything other than books, one might conclude their stocking policy to be their own business. As it is, it can be hailed as censorship should they fail to stock a particular title. For years they did not stock *Private Eye*. I know of at least one bookseller who did not stock the Wicked Willy titles because he considered them in bad taste, and *The Ancient Art of Farting* met a similar fate. For the same reasons, the front of store manager of a major independent bookseller, who had a background of military service, lobbied strongly that its prestigious premises should not be sullied with copies of *Diana, Her True Story*. He was overruled.

6. The permanence of books

Obsolescence is built-in to many commodities today, and it may be a pity that books do not crumble into dust after a few years' inactivity on a shelf ... If books are to play their essential part within the new industry of communication they must win acceptance as living necessities and not as dead relics.

(Sir Robert Lusty, ibid)

There are few items that are bought to last a lifetime, and those that are – for example, jewellery or art – have high price tags to match their expected longevity. Firms of book printers may regret the fact, but the product they produce is still considered in a similar light. The cover price is generally low, yet the public seem to have higher expectations of a book than of other forms of entertainment; they are buying a bit of history.

For instance, it seems to be accepted that children's clothes will reflect current fashions (otherwise they will not wear them), and, depending on price, not last for ever. But when it comes to books, it seems much greater sturdiness is required. To prove this point, Boxtree recently received an angry letter from a parent. After repeated reading, a Thunderbirds book they had purchased for their son had fallen to pieces. Had the backing fallen off a jigsaw, or an arm become inextricably lodged inside one of the turtle fraternity, one suspects that there would have been no complaint, although the same amount of money, or more, would have been spent. Publishers of encyclopedias already stress the longevity of their product. I wonder how long it will be before consumers are informed whether or not the mass market titles they buy are printed on acid-free paper?

7. Books as part of the cultural heritage

Our culture is nourished by a wide range of books being available, not on a profitless search for volume on a limited range of titles.

(Martin Grindley, *Bookseller*, 19 April 1991)

Abolition of retail price maintenance in France was initiated by the Minister of Finance, but its reinstatement was at the intervention of the Minister of Culture. Michael Zifcak says that since resale price maintenance was abolished in Australia, while the number of titles published has not gone down, their quality has. So much so that the Literature Board of Australia (a statutory body acting as adviser to the government on arts) is actively involved in subsidising the publishing of Australian cultural books, either to enable them to be published at all, or at least to be published at prices which will achieve wide readership. The Literature Board for a time also offered promotion subsidies to retail bookshops, paying half the advertising costs on titles promoting Australian creative writing, ie a direct government subsidy.

8. Society's view of the author

Reports are circulating of local councils, keen to fill newly built shopping centres, offering 'reverse premiums' to chain bookstores to encourage them to set up shop. Presumably they do this to offer diversity, interest, and to break the monopoly of shoe shops and building societies. Unfortunately, it seems that the same spirit of welcome does not, in the main, extend to the producers of what is sold – the authors.

Society's view of the author does not, in general, help publishers or booksellers to sell more books. Indeed, people who complain about the price of books often miss the author out of the equation completely. £4.99 is described as 'extortionate' for such a 'thin' book; that is, in terms of cardboard cover, pages and ink, not original thought.

Some nationalities do not consider that original thought should be paid for at all:

> the concept that literature and ideas are free was the basis of the Chinese rejection of copyright – not commercial piracy conducted for private gain, as with the nest of book pirates in Taiwan.
>
> (Alan Hill, *In Pursuit of Publishing*, John Murray, 1988)

The International Intellectual Property Alliance reported that pirates in the 28 countries on its copyright watch list cost US book publishers an estimated $485 million in losses in 1992.

Meanwhile, 'Publishers think of authors as feckless and egomaniac children' (Philip Howard, *The Times*, 29 January 1992) and even those who recognise an author's unavoidable egotism as part of the job ('to keep going at all, an author has to believe that people will want to read what he writes '[Alan Hill]) can find some individual spirits difficult to deal with. The collective opinion of authors, as evinced at meetings of their professional society, seems to be that they are seen as rather a nuisance by their publishers.

The general public's view of the author tends to fall into one of two categories:

(a) the Jeffrey Archer/Frederick Forsyth-type millionaire, who makes easy money and can run off another bestseller in the course of a few weeks. Booker prize winners tend to be viewed in this category too.
(b) the very clever type, for whom the satisfaction of appearing in print is sufficient reward for labour, and writing in poor surroundings is essential to the creative process. To this type of author, money is largely an irrelevance, although it is assumed that appearing on television programmes as an 'expert' brings fat fees.

The reality is less encouraging. A recent survey by the Society of Authors revealed that only around 5 per cent of their members were able to earn their full-time living from writing and, apart from a few 'mega-bucks' writers, the earnings level of those able to do so was not high: around £12,500 per annum for a full-time writer with years of experience.

The advances war of the late 1980s benefited a few highly paid writers but the pendulum has now swung the other way; new advances are being cut back because every book has to contribute more. It is harder than ever for first-time authors to get into print, and those who do earn less. What might have earned an advance of £3000 two years ago is now down to £1500. The amount that the government allocates to distribute to authors to compensate for possible sales lost through library loans is very small. Public Lending Right (PLR) will share out less than £4 million in 1993, whereas the Arts Council is giving £39 million to drama and £36 million to music. Each time you borrow a book from a public library the author receives 1.8p. PLR rewards only the biggest fish with anything reasonable, and no one earns more than £6000.

Author royalties are low – 7.5 – 10 per cent is usual for a book that may have taken years to write. Feedback to the author on the artefact finally produced, too, is limited. Writing is of necessity a solitary occupation. Publishers often base a decision to publish general fiction on preference for one manuscript over another, not fine-tuning of an existing brand or market trend as happens in other sorts of retailing.

But author solidarity is not strong and rivalry is intense: most view their appearance in print as a herald of things to come, and will compromise on payment received. If one author turns down an offer on grounds of an inadequate fee, there will always be someone else around to take the job on.

9. The end of the book is nigh

A growing body of people see books as an irrelevance: in the fast-moving information world, a book is out of date before it is printed. All the information they need can be gained through alphabetic characters, but in formats other than bound: newspaper; microfiche; on-line access to computers:

> what we used to call literacy is today attainable without recourse to any serious reading during a lifetime. The lazy gadgetry of electronic communication can produce a well-informed, intelligent and sophisticated citizen capable of attaining a high standard of living without ever reading a book at all.
>
> (Sir Robert Lusty, ibid)

> they [books] are too slow and they are too boring to fit in with today's life, you know, it just takes too long to read them.
>
> (Dominik Diamond, Presenter of Channel 4's computer game show, *Gamesmaster*, in a phone-in on Radio 4, January 1993)

> the days of the book are numbered ... it's like a timebomb.
>
> (Tony Feldman, Chairman of the world's first conference on electronic books, who describes himself as electronic publishing's most ardent evangelist)

Gadgetry is flourishing. The 'imagination machine' – CD ROM Interactive – is taking off, and the feasibility of a 'Bookbank' has been discussed in the trade press: a huge subscription database which could load individual 'smart cards' (like credit cards) with digitised books. These could then be played back on small, hand-held, electronic 'readers', like lap top computers, with a push button page-turning facility. And once one title is finished, with a subscription, the card can be reloaded at the bookshop or library with another. Even the traditional confines of the London Book Fair were invaded when in March 1993, for the first time in its history, the Fair set up a 'multi-media pavilion', a group of stalls 'displaying hand-held computers which can be read like paperbacks and software which redefines books as all-singing, all-dancing personal communicators' (Susannah Herbert, Arts Correspondent, *Daily Telegraph*, 22 March 1993).

Should all this depress us? Does it spell the long-term end of book publishers? It is certainly true that many publishers are moving into other products: video and CD ROM and investigating new electronic technologies that can retrieve and print on demand. Should both publishers and booksellers increasingly view themselves as purveyors of information in whatever form is most appropriate to the market?

A rather more optimistic view comes from Michael Twyman, Professor of Typography and Graphic Communication at the University of Reading. He cites the existence of certain 'eternal formats' which, once achieved, will not change, and of which the book is one. Although the organisation of the page has changed, and will continue to do so, the basic book format has remained the same for hundreds of years. This seems logical. When your eyes are tired at night, who would prefer a hand-held electronic 'reader' to a paperback that can drop on the floor when you fall asleep? Would you really want to take an electronic device to the beach? Hard-wearing textbooks are unlikely to be replaced in schools by individual pocket computers: think of the cost and theft implications. Cookery books are much easier to work from, and more durable, than odd cuttings clipped from magazines and newspapers, however tasty they sounded and determined you were to add something new to your repertoire.

As Isaac Asimov, the science fiction guru, asked:

> If you could build a small package, something small enough to carry in your coat pocket, a machine which would instantly start and stop, in which you could instantly reverse yourself or go forward, which would require no batteries or other energy sources, and which would provide you with full information on an entire civilisation for around the same price as a bottle of whisky, what would you call it?
>
> A book.

Chapter 6

Market Research and the Book Trade

market research together with the use of other trade or in-house information is integral to the successful decision making of any major consumer-based company today.

(Training handbook of the Market Research Society)

I have been involved with *Books and the Consumer* since its inception. For the entire period I have been continuously asked to define the real value of the research in the reality of the market-place.

(Chris Kirby, Time Life Books 1992)

In this chapter I propose to look at market research and its value to publishers in three ways:

1. What market research is; why it is useful; where to get it.
2. How the book trade can implement useful and cost-effective market research campaigns.
3. Examples of what has come out of publishers' use of market research.

If publishers have a slightly different understanding of marketing compared with the rest of industry (see Chapters 2 and 3), this is fully reflected in their view of market research.

Agreed, market research is a newish trend – most British companies did not start including it in their budgets until the end of the 1970s. But since then management in many manufacturing and servicing companies have realised the benefits of an independent, objective viewpoint and are using external market research companies much more readily.

The book trade carries out little formal market research. Until *very* recently only a few of the most marketing-minded publishers built research into their budgets. Most are not at that stage, even now.

According to the PA, retail sales in 1991 were around £2.5 billion. The amount spent on externally commissioned market research each year is around £0.5 million. (Companies which do spend on market research are generally those approaching specific markets, such as educational and reference, and the work is usually carried out internally rather than using external expertise.)

Around 1 per cent of the membership of the Market Research Society lists publishing as an area of interest, but this largely refers to those involved in magazine production. Within the market research industry the impression received is that publishers are regarded as amateurs in action, ignoring major market opportunities through reliance on tradition and inherited beliefs. One publisher, now imbued with belief in market research, quoted Goethe: 'there is nothing more frightful than ignorance in action.'

This lack of interest in market research can be explained in several ways:

- Market research data about books are thought to be difficult to acquire. To start with, there is no agreement about how many books are actually being sold.

  For what other major industry are brand leaders or sales by outlet actually in real doubt?
  (Trevor Glover, managing director, Penguin Group, keynote speech, Books and the Consumer Conference, 18 February 1993)

In the car or drugs industries, individual member firms provide sales data to show how their various products are selling, and hence overall industry performance can accurately be seen. In the book trade, while most PA members, and some firms (eg Reed) who are not members, do supply sales information to the PA, there is no requirement so to do, and in any case subsequent bookshop returns can skew the figures. The PA's industry estimates are thus based on weighted averages, according to past experience and individual publishing sector activity. Other compilers of sales information such as Business Monitor and Euromonitor tend to show lower sales levels, to be less optimistic.

- Second, it is assumed that such market research data would not be helpful in trying to predict future demand in a creative industry.

  Market research is very little used in publishing and it is easy to understand why: it's expensive, and in a creative industry one fears that consumer attitudes might simply stifle imagination. How can they possibly contribute to better writing and better books?
  (Rupert Lancaster of Fodor; introduction to an article on how market research can be both effectively and profitably used, *Bookseller*, 25 January 1991)

- As each book is a different product, market research would arguably need to be commissioned for each title. The low purchase price and sheer volume of titles being handled by each house would make this impossible, both financially and practically. The obvious answer is research by brand or imprint, but too often the idea stalls on the 'each book is unique' argument.

- The risks in the book industry are smaller. In the world outside publishing, marketing specialists claim that 80 per cent of new products fail, hence the importance of thorough market research before investment. For the book trade investment in individual products is mostly on a much lower scale, and so overall exposure to risk is much reduced; the gap between success and failure is much smaller.

  John Samuels, managing director of the British Market Research Bureau, commented that less than 0.2 per cent of the cost of production is typically spent by manufacturing companies on market research. Publishing in the UK may be a £2.5 billion industry but that spend is fragmented between many different companies and products; 0.2 per cent of the production costs of most individual houses would buy relatively little research.

- Publishers already know (or think they know) it all. But the internal information sources on which most publishers rely tell them little about how their products are perceived in the market-place, even less about the reasons why some fail, and there is little exploration of how different targeting might be more productive. As one market research expert commented: 'publishers are more concerned with trade relationships than marketing to consumers'.

1. What market research is; why it is useful; where to get it

Market research is designed to provide information which assists companies in determining their product development and marketing strategies and tactics, including exploration of current or potential markets and strategies. It helps to reduce uncertainty, monitor performance and make decisions. A programme of market research helps companies to:

- assess the market and marketing opportunities and threats;
- investigate strengths and weaknesses in companies, and their products/services;
- devise appropriate products and marketing strategies to meet them;
- obtain feedback on how the plans are working;
- devise reasoned and appropriate plans for the future.

In other words, market research helps to show where a company's resources and efforts should be concentrated for most effect. It aims to understand the market in order to sell more effectively to it.

Like publishing, this area of marketing has developed its own jargon. Here are a few buzz-words. With effective market research a company can understand:

- *market segmentation* (groups of consumers with similar needs, separable by social grade, demographic, ethnographic, psychographic factors and so on);
- how to offer a *competitive advantage* (what they can offer to the customer that makes their product or service better or more appealing than that of their competitors);
- *positioning* (a combination of the first two terms; where and how they will compete).

It is also vital to understand the difference between the two most important sorts of market research: qualitative and quantitative.

Qualitative market research tries to establish breadth of feeling towards a particular product or service (how does the market feel about it?). *Quantitative* market research tries to count (how big is the actual/potential market; how many people are aware of the need; how well is the advertising about the product getting through?). These two sorts of market research may be used in combination; for example, qualitative research for establishing the criteria for selection, quantitative for counting reasons and classifying the market into different segments, socio-economic groups and so on. In terms of spending, more money is spent on quantitative than qualitative research.

Market research is only useful if you:

- are precise about what you want to know (research revealing absolutely everything about a market would probably not be possible or useful, and certainly not affordable!);
- pay attention to trends that are identified;
- accept that although market research can be used successfully for short-term tactical purposes, it probably works best if you are willing to take a long-term view of your company and its products. The companies which make the best use of research are those which build research into their planning and marketing processes, and do not only use it as a means of obtaining answers to short-term problems.

Market research can identify various different kinds of information:

1. Performance data (what is happening in the market?)
   (a) Market research

- who buys what and in what quantity?
- market size
- market growth/contraction
- is the market contactable/accessible?

(b) Product research
- which products are being bought (bestselling versus others)?
- in what quantities?
- how fast are they selling?
- what are the buying patterns by market segment?
- what is the usage (how are they used, how do they perform)?
- what are trade purchase and stock levels?
- what are the distribution levels?

(c) Marketing/promotional research
- how can the appropriate messages be best put across?

2. Behavioural, attitudinal and motivational data

(a) Behavioural data
- who is buying and not buying?
- what sizes/variations are being bought?
- where are they bought?
- why are they bought (how will they be used)?
- what are the shopping habits/spending power of those buying?

(b) Attitude and motivational data
- identifying how the choice is actually made by the market; what are the key and secondary influences?
- what are the perceived benefits that the product or service offers?
- what is the reaction from the market to company image/offers?

Sources of information for market research

(a) *Personal experience*. Do you know members of the primary market personally – customers and potential customers? Do you know where they get together? Can you go along and talk to them or to those who buy on their behalf?

(b) *Internal records (existing performance data)*, eg customer lists; accounts department statistics; sales levels; reports from reps; customer letters/complaints/warranty claims etc. Can these be analysed and quantified into trends?

(c) *Published information*. There is a range of information that is both available and relevant, even if not specifically applicable to target markets, eg government statistics and surveys; industry association sources; membership of cooperative industry research surveys. Such information may be purchased or is sometimes available free.

(d) *Formal and specialist market research*, in-house through allocating new or existing members of staff; externally through dedicated agencies or specialists; sometimes a combination of the two.

Do not assume that in-house is always cheaper (although in practice the costs may be culled from several contributing budgets. External services offer the advantage of trained personnel, dedicated to this kind of work; they should be objective and free from preconceived ideas about a particular market or opportunity. Few publishers have any experience of designing appropriate market research vehicles to find out what they want to know. Similarly, sensitivity or security may indicate that it is better to use an external organisation and screen the identity of an interested party.

Different methods of market research

There are various different methods of conducting market research; their respective value depends on the nature of the population (of 'owners', 'users', 'buyers' and 'influencers' eg schoolteachers) being targeted and the most effective method of reaching them. The sampling group for the test is decided on and then usually achieved either by quota ('20 per cent of my sample must be under the age of 20 ...') or random (manual or computer-generated sampling list) methods. Quota methods are more commonly used as they are considerably cheaper. Alternatively, the interviewer may select those to be questioned through a process of self-qualification; for example, a product they have just bought. Questions are then asked through:

- telephone surveys;
- questionnaires completed by individuals (either conducted house-to-house, or delivered/handed out with a purchase, and then completed in the recipient's own time and returned either by post or through electronic transfer);
- a research project consisting of in-store interviews or household surveys;
- 'mall' or 'hall' tests;
- group discussions;
- panel research (a group of people are recruited to provide information from time to time either on an *ad hoc* or more formal basis, such as the BBC Radio's Panel of Listeners).

How cost effective is market research?

Market research is normally only cost effective if it is designed carefully to meet the specific needs at the time (often marketing or sales or product development), and the resulting conclusions are acted upon. Data for data's sake is rarely worthwhile; it is better to plan the collection of information into a continuous marketing information system.

Wasted market research (usually information greeted with 'so what!') can usually be put down to one of the following avoidable reasons:

- inadequate briefing;
- inappropriate survey design;
- neglect of available information sources;
- poor communications;
- biased interpretation;
- lack of ownership of the survey/data. Somebody should want it done and act as the sponsor.

2. How the book trade can implement useful and cost-effective market research campaigns

If the book trade has, in the past, purchased little market research information, and commissioned even less, there are still several existing information sources that should be investigated.

Sources of market research for publishers

(a) Personal experience

Scanning the shelves in bookshops and talking to members of the target audience (eg attending their conferences and professional organisation meetings) help to build up information about the market for books.

(b) Internal records

Individual publishers can tap in-house sources to find out what has been published in the past few years that is similar; year-on-year statistics; mailing responses from previous campaigns; telemarketing (in- and outbound); the level of returns; feedback from the reps and the distribution centre all yield information.

Some booksellers have information from EPOS and other stock monitoring systems to tell them what is selling fastest and spot trends, although not all retailers are equally expert at using it!

(c) Published information

Despite a general belief in the industry that market research is hard to come by, there are several published sources, both book-dedicated and book-related.

Articles in the trade press, newspapers and professional journals, and data in reference books provide much information. Then there is a variety of different information assembled for one use but relevant to another. For example, reports on the fastest growing subjects for students at GCSE and A level would be useful to an educational publisher; 'medical briefing' information in the quality press shows where relevant publishers should be looking for growing markets for their prestigious journals.

The government's Business Monitor figures provide consistent data from 1983 on revenue (although not all categories of books are detailed). Information is also available from a number of research agencies, as well as book trade organisations such as Book Tokens, the PA, the BA and Whitaker's. The *Bookseller's* list of titles goes back to 1975, the Publishers Association statistics scheme covers the 1980s and early 1990s, and edited statistical trends are regularly issued by them (eg *Book Publishing in the UK: Key Facts 1990* (covers the years 1981 – 89) and *The PA Book Trade Year Book 1992*).

There are also many regular surveys from those producing industry commentaries. Mintel, Euromonitor and the Government Household Surveys are of great value, as are similar studies from other countries.

(d) Formal and specialist market research

The publishing industry has a dedicated research organisation providing industry information (Book Marketing Ltd) and also benefits from the specialist services of a number of other general agencies, mostly on an *ad hoc* basis. For example, Strategy, Research and Action Ltd have made a point of serving a specialist sector of the publishing market, with both tailor-made and syndicate-funded research. Most large agencies (Gallup, NOP, SRA etc) run regular cooperative questionnairing programmes aimed at both general and specific markets (such as household or children's interests), and these have sometimes included publishing questions, mostly from magazine publishers. BMRB International run the Target Group Index (TGI) which is a survey of about 24,000 households, asking about their purchase of a wide range of products and services, use of the varied media and lifestyle. Books and reading form a small section in this.

The role of Book Marketing Ltd (BML)

Book Marketing Ltd started life as the Book Marketing Council of the Publishers Association, for which PA members paid an additional fee. *Books and the Consumer*, a detailed and on-going report into book buying, borrowing and reading habits was started under these auspices in 1988. With the review of PA subscriptions and what should be provided for

111

them in 1990, the Book Marketing Council was closed down and an independent company, Book Marketing Ltd, set up. This has now entered its fourth year of trading under managing director Clare Harrison. Many publishers feel comfortable using this service as it is run by people who understand the industry, supported by the expertise of non-publisher specialists, and fees are pitched at the industry's level.

BML offers a unique range of specialist marketing services to the book industry.

1. Books and the Consumer

Around 18 participant companies continue to fund the most comprehensive consumer book survey in existence, which achieves 1800 interviews per year and a wealth of data, both panoramic and specific for individual sectors of the market.

Such syndicated research can be much more cost effective than individual commissions, but BML are quick to point out that this does not mean it has to be too generalised to benefit both multi-imprint customers and individual companies with specialist interests, or that it denies individual subscribers a competitive advantage. BML have devoted time to explaining to clients how to use and benefit from the data on offer, and there is a telephone hotline for help in analysing and interpreting the figures. For the past four years research findings have been presented alongside examples of how individual subscribers can benefit from the information. Clients can add specific questions of their own to the interviewing ('bolt-on' research), which are confidential to them, and give them the chance to cross-analyse the results with all the other questions on the questionnaire.

2. Individual research commissions

BML has an extensive database of information on the book trade and the consumer, probably the most comprehensive available. This is tapped by in-house market research professionals who offer a tailor-made consultancy service. Sometimes the information required extends beyond desk research and needs dedicated or primary research of a quantitative or qualitative nature. Most of the commissions are confidential in nature, but the following give a flavour:

- A year-long study for the Arts Council on the impact of author events on books sales and consumer attitudes. This was carried out using a variety of different methods from questionnaires on seats to face-to-face interviews.
- Pre-publication research for Orion on new cover designs for the

re-launch of the paperback Everyman, a well-established literary fiction series. This was done mainly through group discussions with consumers.
- A market segmentation study for a major reference publisher, involving interviews in retail markets, in educational/institutional establishments and with consumers buying in bookshops.
- Research into the market for books on tape for Random Century. This included consumer research, and research in both the mainstream book trade and non-traditional outlets.
- Various niche market studies including one on the market for baby books in the UK and Europe.

3. Publications

BML produces monthly *Book Marketing Updates*, digests of new and original research data. These are available on subscription or free to clients. Other publications include *Book Facts*, a comprehensive annual compendium of statistical information culled from over 50 sources on the book trade; one-off research reports on different aspects of the market (eg on books as gifts, the travel market, children's books, the impact and effectiveness of author events); and trade and consumer catalogues (eg Catalogue of Maps and Travel Guides).

4. Other services

These include specialist seminars, conferences and workshops. BML also runs promotions and organises the National Book Sale.

3. Examples of what has come out of publishers' use of market research

The *Lost Sales* survey 1980 (LSS)

Commissioned by the Book Marketing Council when it was still part of the PA, and carried out before the high street expansion of Dillons or the founding of Waterstones (1982), the LSS still makes interesting reading today. The emphasis it placed on the potential for exploring the market for books as gifts, and the value of the impulse buyer in bookshops, accurately predicted some of the work that BML is now doing.

Information revealed by the BML *Books and the Consumer* Survey

- *Reading habits.* At any one time just under half of all adults are likely to be reading a book for pleasure. On average, people who read books devote just over eight hours of their week to this activity. Over half of all adults have a library ticket, half of whom borrow at least once a month, the rest less often. (This optimistic view – too many people assume that television has replaced reading – was confirmed in a survey by Carrick James Market Research in February 1991, which showed that 61 per cent of youngsters aged between 5 and 18 read for pleasure with 41 per cent having done so in the past week.)

– *What percentage of the population buy new books?* It is time to update the notion that only a small élite buy new books: only 20 per cent of the sample interviewed in 1992 had *not* bought books during the previous year, and in terms of numbers of purchasers, the recession has had no effect in the four-year period 1989 – 92.

Percentage of total sample buying books each year

1989	1990	1991	1992
78%	77%	81%	80%

– *Who are the heavy book buyers?* Those buying at least 16 books a year make up 27 per cent of the adult population but buy almost three-quarters of books sold; 73 per cent of books are bought by 27 per cent of the market. In the main, heavy book buyers are found in social grouping AB, and there is a strong correlation between high income and high expenditure on books. But it is important to remember that while the ABs buy most books, they are not the only buying group, as the chart below shows. ABs are also the smallest part of the social spectrum – groups C and D together make up 60 per cent of the population.

Demographic profile of paperback and hardback buyers

Social grade	% of new paperback buyers for self in last 12 months	% of new hardback buyers for self in last 12 months	% of adult pop.*
AB	20	22	17.8
C1	29	30	23.9
C2	29	27	27.8
DE	22	21	30.5

Source: Books and the Consumer (1992)
*Estimated adult population (15+)
Source: JICNARS National Readership Survey, July 1990 – June 1991, based on the individual grade of head of household.

Terminal education age is also a key factor in influencing levels of book purchasing, as is the amount of reading done as a child. The 25 – 44s are the key age group for book buying; they make up 36 per cent of the population but buy over half of all consumer books purchased by adults in the UK. More women buy books than men.

- *Which newspapers reach most book buyers?* The papers which would reach the highest number of heavy book buyers are the *Sun* and the *News of the World*, although the highest proportions of heavy book buyers are found among the readers of the 'quality' dailies. More heavy book buyers can be reached through Radio 1 or commercial radio than listeners to Radio 3 and 4, although again the percentage of listeners who are heavy book buyers for the latter is higher.

  But most promotional activity is restricted to a narrow range of media appealing to middle-class readers. ABC1s are more likely to be influenced by book reviews, advertisements and seeing or hearing publicity, C2DEs by hearing that a book has been adapted into a film, TV or radio programme, or is about to be.

- *Who buys by post, and does this mean that sales are lost to retail outlets?* One in five adults buy books by post and three in four from retail outlets. Women buy almost twice as many books by post as men. Postal buyers are most likely to be AB, enjoy reading, have over 500 books, and have children in the family under the age of 11. They are attracted to buying by post by an introductory offer, cheaper or better value for money and convenience.

  But postal buyers do not buy exclusively by direct mail; they are mostly heavy book buyers who will buy from any source. Twenty-two per cent of book buyers buy by post, but only 12 per cent of books are bought in this way.)

- *The market for books bought as gifts it huge* (it is estimated to be worth 40 per cent of books bought by adults) and not yet fully exploited by either publishers or booksellers. It is not a niche market or an AB socio-economic grouping, and is equally split between children's and adults' books, maps, atlases and guides.

- *Price of books.* Nearly nine out of ten paperback buyers regard paperbacks as very or fairly good value; one in four as very good value. Seven out of ten hardback buyers feel that they represent good value for money, one in four very good value. However, in comparison with other products, paperbacks have started to seem more expensive (35 per cent of sample thought so in 1989, 41 per cent in 1991).

- *Do libraries curb sales?* No. Frequent users of libraries are more likely to be frequent book buyers, and the survey identified those who visit a library every two to three weeks as most likely to buy books as well as

115

borrow. Those who borrow many books at a time (regardless of the frequency with which they use their library tickets) tend also to buy more books than average. Those who use libraries also, on average, buy more books to give as presents.

The great majority of those who do not use a library do not buy books either. Schemes that have linked promotional projects in libraries with local bookshops (for example, *Well Worth Reading)* have reported markedly increased sales. East Sussex tried selling books in libraries and found it worked. (Public Lending Right has, in any case, revealed that the nature of books bought from bookshops differs from the kind of book typically borrowed by a library user.)

The wealth of information from the *Books and the Consumer* survey to my mind fully answers the question about whether or not market research is useful to publishers.

Other examples of market research in practice

Dorling Kindersley spend a lot of money on market research, although this is largely carried out by their own staff rather than by an external market research company. More significantly, market research is regarded by DK as an integral part of producing a book, not a luxury to be bought only in the case of particularly important projects. Staff work in small teams on particular areas of publishing, and all members, marketing, editorial and design, are involved in the research or, as it is usually referred to in-house, 'developing the idea'.

For DK, market research consists of wide consultation with as many people as possible who are likely to be able to predict the success of a publishing idea.

An elaborate dummy of each proposed book costs between £5000 and £10,000; up to £80,000 on a series. These incorporate live (not Latin) text; show how illustrations work and the pages relate to each other. This is then shown to the firm's 30-plus overseas area managers (around 75 per cent of any book's total sales are likely to be made abroad), UK sales representatives, trade contacts and retail advisers. The company reckons that 'nagging at an idea until it is right' pays off in the long run in higher sales and better market penetration. Sales of the books subsequently produced are extremely high, and most books go to print with almost the entire print run pre-sold. It is thought that no DK book has ever been remaindered.

Market research in educational publishing is comparatively easy because the market is definable, locatable and quantifiable.

Oxford University Press, for example, regularly run direct mail questionnaires and telephone questionnaires for customer research, and then send trialling scripts to schools for product research. It is easy to access existing customers these days through the customer databases created by direct supply to schools. And it is usually the subject editor who runs this research, so the editor learns from direct contact with the end user.

It should be said that the objective of this kind of customer research is to determine *how* the book should be published, ie establishing customer preferences at the present time for particular formats or approaches, to help the publisher create competitive advantage. What should be published is determined by the publisher's research into curriculum developments at a government level, and informed anticipation of future trends.

In 1990 *Fodor*, who were part of the Map, Atlas and Travel Guide Research Group, run by Strategy, Research and Action Ltd (see page 165), commissioned some market research on travel guides. They believed their books were capable of doing better, but felt they did not know enough about the market or the customers.

Using a combination of holiday industry statistics and their own independent research, they were able to identify and understand better the independent holiday maker.

Holiday statistics showed that there are about 5 million independent travellers, but the research group data revealed a further 7 million people who travel abroad on package holidays, but do not want to lie on the beach all day. In other words, their market was over 100 per cent larger than they had expected.

These independent travellers take time to plan their itineraries and read about their destinations; they are not tied to the school holidays or even the summer (about a third of holidays are taken during the winter months). Fodors used this information to liaise with the book trade, to provide better targeted point of sale in shops, for longer periods. They also arranged special promotions with several outlets featuring relevant sponsorship.

Mills and Boon commissioned market research as far back as 1982 to find out who their readers were. I remember hearing a fascinating talk at the Society of Young Publishers that year, when it was revealed that, far from the accepted market profile of M&B readers as bored housewives with time on their hands, the company's customers were to be found to be in every sector of female society: from barristers to barmaids, from directors to dishwashers.

Today the company uses research to:

ensure we offer books our customers want, to develop new titles and new markets and thus to help us offer consistently high quality and varied series, to cater for different tastes and to continue to grow in the market place.

(Heather Walton, Marketing Director, Mills and Boon, BML Conference 18 February 1993)

For example, Mills and Boon use the *Books and the Consumer* survey, in combination with their own reader research, to try to establish which series will appeal to which market sectors and why. The large sample provided by the survey, and the chance to compare and contrast the data with the company's own in-house information on readers, means that it can help to target M&B buyers (rather than the total market), identify potential new segments and establish new product or market categories.

Having identified a market segment which is of interest, an idea can then be further explored through concept research (perhaps through group discussions with carefully selected people, to establish what potential buyers actually think of an idea and develop it into a saleable product); quantitative research (mainly through questionnaires and interviewing to establish how many people are likely to respond favourably, and to make inferences about the target market as a whole); and testing (often by means of product placement with potential buyers). Subsequent monitoring of a product in the market-place provides an on-going check on quality control and permits changes to be made, if necessary, as a series progresses.

 For individual research needs – for example, testing unusual storylines or delicate subjects – and to see what the reaction is likely to be from regular/infrequent/possible new readers, the company will try to take a 'dipstick sounding'. This is done using a variety of different techniques: inserts in books; contacting competition entrants; readers' letters; press monitoring; *ad hoc* research and trade feedback.

With the crime fiction market buoyant, in 1985 *HarperCollins* found sales of their brand leader Agatha Christie were declining – by around 1 per cent a year. Market research was commissioned from James R Adams and Associates to find out why, and a mixture of desk research, qualitative and quantitative research was suggested.

The market for her titles was found to be biased towards the young, the better educated and those from higher socio-economic groups. Group discussions among existing Christie readers and current paperback buyers were set up; views from all socio-economic grades and both sexes were sought. The aims of these groups were to establish how both potential and actual Christie readers viewed crime in relation to other genres, and to establish Christie's particular position within the genre. Group respondents were also shown cover designs, which had changed significantly over 20 years.

The most interesting finding to emerge from the research was that Christie readers like the 'niceness' of the crimes; there may be a whole series of violent deaths in her books, but there is no dwelling on the details. However, the current range of rather gory covers (influenced by the growing horror market) put these readers off. As a direct result, new cover designs, both intriguing and subtle, were commissioned and a new promotion of Agatha Christie as the 'Queen of Crime', supported by information on the research, received widespread support from the book trade. In the first year after making the changes, paperback sales increased by 40 per cent (1 million up to 1.4 million units).

In 1987, after a difficult period, and under new management, *Cassell* commissioned some market research from BRMB. Although the firm had not published a new dictionary for several years, they realised that their name was still widely associated with this kind of product, and decided to test it out.

A wide sample of interviewees, designed to be representative of all adults in Great Britain, was asked a variety of questions. After identifying which publishers produce dictionaries they were asked to estimate the respective qualities of the products on offer (eg price, how comprehensive, up-to-date and so on); in other words, to discuss the power of brand images in the market-place. Results were broken down by sex, age, social grade and television area. Interviewees were then asked a variety of other questions about their dictionary purchasing habits (how often, who for, what they already owned, reasons for choice and so on). Results showed that the name of Cassell was well associated with dictionaries, although new dictionary publishing had not been a priority for many years; and that their dictionaries were particularly well regarded for their comprehensive and up-to-date content. The management developed from this the plan to stress the wider notion of all their works' reliability and accuracy, as well as the decision to invest in new dictionaries.

Conclusion

It is probably true that publishers cannot, and in most cases should not, afford individually commissioned market research campaigns for specific titles. But 'bestsellers' – books which may be expected to generate large sales and significant income – may well benefit from research into such areas as jacket design, promotional campaigns and so on. And for all titles, the use made of in-house sources, in particular when projected titles are still at concept stage, could be greatly increased.

There is, too, much general industry information on customers and markets that could help to improve marketing, on all sides of the trade. For example, market research has shown that the value for money that books offer should be stressed; that more promotions should be targeted at markets other than the ABs; that the potential for selling books as gifts is enormous and that everyone involved should monitor the effects of their marketing much more carefully. Similarly, publishers are now realising that they should research their brands or imprints, as they appreciate more the importance of creating consumer awareness to achieve 'pull through' via sales outlets.

Chapter 7

Distribution, Customer Care and Other Services

Distribution is the bridge that links publishers and their market. Neglect it and you will never get to grips with your market.

(Desmond Clarke, Managing Director, International Thomson Publishing Services Ltd (ITPS))

Wider industry has long regarded distribution as an indispensable part of the marketing equation: there is little point in producing goods and stimulating demand if they are not in the shops when customers want to buy them. Publishers, in general, have been slow to accept this message, but the fact that most firms *do* now heed its importance, still does not mean that all in the garden is rosy.

The whole area of distribution is one steeped in trade controversy; no other subject arouses such bitterness and readiness to hurl abuse. (The NBA debate attracts much discussion, but for the most part sides are more established and consist of Dillons and [closet] supporters versus the rest.)

> The arguments over book distribution are so well rehearsed and opinion so entrenched that progress has seemed impossible against what has been a background of mutual recrimination.
>
> (*Bookseller*, 10 May 1991)

Distribution, too, definitely remains at the non-sexy, 'dogsbody end of the business' (Giles Clark). Warehouse premises are usually far from the metropolis and its associated hype, and staff are often made to feel, or just do feel, alienated from the 'real' business of publishing. Today prestige is slowly improving, and even if few people join publishing companies in order to pursue a career in distribution, it is accepted that knowledge of how a company's systems work is an asset for those aspiring to senior management.

How long distribution takes or should take

There is an industry-wide perception that publishers are not good at distributing their titles. Working parties assemble and report their findings, and there are regular laments in the trade press about how long it all takes. Some firms have improved their performance dramatically, but still, if you order a title in a bookshop, and the title has to be ordered from the publisher rather than a wholesaler, you will often be quoted two to three weeks to be 'on the safe side'.

So how long is too long? In 1990, a survey by the BA found that the average time from bookseller's order to receipt of books had fallen from 13.3 working days in 1981 to 8.5 days in 1985, and was up to 8.6 days in 1990, ie about a week and a half allowing for weekends. Wholesalers, who are able to insist on a minimum order quantity or order value, average 1.8 working days. When timing is really critical, for example, at Christmas or at the start of the academic year, there are often special arrangements set up by publishers: hotlines with a guaranteed delivery within 48 hours.

Those who have worked in other industries are surprised to hear such figures criticised, and even more surprised to find that stock items can be ordered in single copies rather than 'outer packs' (usually with a minimum order quantity of 12 or 18), at relatively low invoice value, without penalty or a special delivery charge, and then subsequently returned if they do not sell.

> If only suppliers for all other goods advertised could offer the service that publishers and book distributors do, we would all be much happier shoppers.
>
> (Annette Footman-Williams, letter to the *Bookseller*, 8 March 1991)

My own experience of the retail trade, when trying to obtain non-stock items, from department or other brand name stores, has been similar to the book trade – two weeks minimum (and often much more). In the USA it was recently reported that the delivery time for durable goods is eight days to industrial consumers, and 11 days to individual consumers.

Book industry working parties have looked at the problems of distribution, and in particular special customer orders for non-stock titles. In 1982 there was a Small Orders Working Party, and in 1991 a group of booksellers, publishers, wholesalers and representatives from the PA and BA issued a report, *Profit by Partnership*, which recommended a nine working day standard from ordering to receipt of books by the shop. Their target was cautious because they were aiming to provide a minimum acceptable standard, to encourage those publishers who consistently fall below this, and thereby damage the whole industry's reputation, to get their act together. Others worried that this just gave everyone a lower goal to aim at, or questioned whether a standard is appropriate when such diversity of buying levels exists. For example, does a firm order for a dump bin full of the latest blockbusting novel, at a huge discount, by a chain bookshop, have much in common with a university campus bookshop's sale or return order for a high price textbook? (The working party's report was not, in any case, endorsed by the PA, essentially because they believe service requirements and standards should be established by individual publishers and booksellers as required by their markets and customers.)

So why is the subject of distribution so fraught with difficulty? Basically because it takes in its path so many trade prejudices, and reflects a 'them and us' attitude between publishers and booksellers. It also highlights the economic problems of serving the book-buying public through a complicated network of large and small bookshops with a vast range of published titles.

The common ground

Both parties have to deal with similar problems – a returnable product with a pre-printed price is unusual today. Both high street shelves and technologically advanced warehouses are expensive places to store books. At the same time, product price is relatively low and product availability extensive. Books have the further disadvantage, in distribution economics, of being relatively heavy for their price. In fact, they have one of the poorest value : weight ratios among consumer goods, making the cost of distributing them in small quantities expensive.

Where publishers and booksellers differ is in their understanding of how the costs of distribution should be allocated. Should speedy distribution be paid for out of the publisher's existing profit margin, ie provided to booksellers as a right, or should it be the product of partnership, regarded as an investment in which all parties share?

The two sides

I saw a postcard in someone's kitchen the other day. It showed a woman's face and the thought bubble read: 'I must keep shopping. I know my life will work out if I can just find the perfect outfit.' There seems to me to be a degree of similar desperation and unreality about the way some, usually smaller booksellers, isolate the issue of distribution time. If all publishers were able to deliver within one week would the trade really be, as the BA has claimed, a 'happier and more profitable place'. Would all the other problems and pressures faced by small bookshops disappear as sales dramatically improved? Or would this just help to prop up the inefficient?

Frustrated *booksellers* feel a two-week turnaround typifies an 'attitude' among publishers. Publishers are accused of making monopolistic use of their position: the bookseller cannot go elsewhere to buy (except to a wholesaler for more popular titles).

Many booksellers cannot see why, if publishers can provide a 48 to 72-hour service on some orders, under certain promotional initiatives, this should not be the standard service available. They see items still on order, when a customer is there in the shop wanting to buy them, as lost sales, for which they blame the publishers.

They resent what they often regard as a second-rate service on offer to small accounts, and think most publishers are complacent about the whole problem. In the late summer of 1989 the BA sent a questionnaire on distribution to 68 publishers and distributors. Only 22 (less than a third) replied. At about the same time, a survey of 42 publishers by Peat Marwick McLintock found that 71 per cent thought they provided a satisfactory service to bookshops.

Booksellers who do not use teleordering complain that the spate of publisher mergers and acquisitions has left them with no clear picture of whom orders should be sent to. They resent the inexact book information put out by publishers. Publishers' invoiced prices are often higher than the book price information supplied to Whitaker's and teleordering and, what is more, they do not seem to think accuracy particularly important. Terms are inadequate, in general, and specifically to cover the cost of spotting and correcting of mistakes. Why should publishers gamble on paying record advances yet 'penny pinch' on surcharges and reliable distribution?

Overseas booksellers complain of publishers' sales and credit management teams not talking to each other; that information about special discounts or extended credit periods is not passed on. The importance of supplying correct information for Teleordering and Book Data is seen even more overseas; the gap between prices on the Whitaker database and invoices can make a nonsense of previous buying decisions.

Publishers know that distribution requires significant capital expenditure in property, computerisation and material handling systems. They do not take a long time to supply books out of sheer bloody-mindedness, but because instant turnaround is so expensive, and often unprofitable. They resent the fact that many booksellers are unwilling to invest themselves; for example, through installing teleordering or even just using first-class stamps for orders. They dislike the:

'begging bowl philosophy which continues to afflict small booksellers'

and agree with Martin Grindley of Browsers Bookshop that they should
'... stop carping and start investing'

(*Bookseller*, 2 November 1990)

Publishers fear that booksellers are confusing their undoubtedly quick
requirement for special orders, and for stock at certain times of the year,
with basic shop stock that should be better managed and reordered with
the publishers' turnaround times in mind. They accuse booksellers of
sending in uneconomic, unconsolidated orders; often handwritten illegibly
with no bibliographical information to enable the titles required to be
identified (it is *they* who pay for the staff to ring shops and find out what
is really wanted). And, after all this effort to get the right titles to the right
shops, the books are sometimes returned.

Them and us

The publishers may be seen as complacent but, on the other side, one can
only describe as extremely grudging the attitude of many booksellers to
good distribution. Christmas 1990 was seen as a good demonstration of
publishers' distribution systems, with no shortages of key titles. When
asked for his opinion of how things had gone, a major bookseller replied:
'As far as I know we had no major complaints.' Clearly, this was the reply
of someone who indicates agreement with an 'I don't have a difficulty with
that' rather than a 'yes', and is sadly, typical. Similarly, once the huge public
interest in *Diana, Her True Story* became clear, instead of greeting with
enthusiasm the publication of a title that was getting new customers into
bookshops, most of the trade's effort seemed to go into cataloguing the
problems, mostly due to low subscription levels. Lost sales through missed
opportunities cost the publishers, who had borne all the initial investment
costs, far more than the retail trade.

The only retail group actively to encourage publishers is the College and
University Booksellers Group which has regularly rewarded ITPS and
OUP with its Golden Parcel Award 'for the speed and quality of its
services'. It was they too who recently pointed out that, for an increasing
number of bookshops, the future of the trade is about more than just single
issues. Just as publishers are today more concerned with providing a complete service to gain competitive advantage, so:

> While a hard core of booksellers kept crying 'terms', most recognised
> that a mix of reducing overheads, improving margins through widening
> the product range, and driving sales more actively, should be given
> priority.

(Report of 21st annual College and University Booksellers Group conference)

125

So, 'distribution' consists of more than just counting days from bookseller order to receipt of books. And although the wide availability of reading material in bookshops benefits society in general, the trade faces high street realities in seeking to fulfil expectations. It is worth looking at the various issues involved in more detail.

Publisher investment in distribution, as a marketing asset not a cost burden

Publishers who have invested heavily in distribution systems, such as Random House, ITPS, Penguin (all of whom were nominated as Distributor of the Year in 1991) and OUP resent being lumped in with the inefficient. There have been suggestions that a premier division of distributors should be advertised, or that publishers' average delivery times should be shown in brackets beside all the titles in the bestseller lists, ie showing quotable delivery times rather than industry averages.

How has this investment been made? In general, and in common with many other industries, there has been a move away from running several distribution centres in different countries, relying instead on a single warehouse, and much improved international transport facilities. For example, instead of making different distribution deals in different countries with carriers or forwarders, publishers are starting to forge links with pan-European and international delivery networks such as Securicor, DHL and Federal Express.

Precise data control systems link sales location and distribution centre and minimise in-house service times. Stock can be sold and invoiced in New York and delivered from the UK, invoiced in US dollars, and the method (and therefore speed) of despatch agreed at the time of sale. The penalties for error increase with distance, so much effort has been placed on quality management, to ensure accuracy and reliability to precise performance standards.

Communications are vastly improved. There is a growing integrated electronic ordering network within Europe, linking any bookseller with every publisher, of whatever nationality. This started with links between the British Teleordering system and Dutch and French systems. (There is a need for international standardisation of procedures and formats, supported by the book trade's professional organisations.)

But this revolution is not just about technology – competitors can catch up and install similarly efficient systems – but about increasing customer orientation. Companies who invest in distribution are also placing emphasis on the *in*tangible aspects of the way they do business, in order to satisfy their customers and increase market share.

Looking to the future, the technological possibilities are far-reaching: electronic ordering and invoicing; the automation of many warehouse functions and wide application of machine readable codes, at warehouse and point of sale – all providing desk top information to those planning future marketing campaigns. Further ahead, developments in electronic printing and copying will gradually change the economics of printing and the structure of stocks held in bulk warehouses.

Much of this is still in the future, but a fundamental question is relevant now: should it be the publishers alone who shoulder the costs of this technological revolution? Should booksellers be demanding state of the art distribution without being willing to share in the costs? Every year for the past few years it is estimated that computer capacity has doubled and prices halved. Yet even now booksellers are only gradually 'wiring up'. In September 1989, a BA survey found that only about 12 per cent of bookshops had any kind of EPOS (electronic point of sale). In 1987 the comparable figure had been between 10 and 11 per cent; by autumn 1991 it was close to 25 per cent. Is this, as Sydney Davis, BA trade practice executive hailed it, 'a staggering increase', or still a disappointing reflection on an only quarter-computerised industry?

The amount of risk taken by the retail trade

Stock levels

At the most basic operating level, a bookshop manager can stock core titles and provide a book-ordering point with little risk. The manager of a stock-holding bookshop, on the other hand, may invest in stock, share the risk, serve the public better and hence stand to make more profit. At the moment, established trade terms fail to differentiate sufficiently between the two activities.

EPOS, the recession and other factors, such as the cutback of institutional purchasing, have undoubtedly meant that bookshops are holding less stock. (In the PMM survey already mentioned, 53 per cent of publishers felt EPOS had a negative effect on stock holdings.)

It is interesting to examine the role of the bookshop *buyer* in this context. The main responsibility of the buyer in industry is to keep a company supplied, but carry the minimum of inventory, for obviously the more stock held, the more cash is tied up. For small, inexpensive items, it is often not worth keeping stock in-house, as the cost of keeping and counting them will outweigh usefulness or value.

In other retail buying sectors such as clothes or jewellery, buyers deal in specialised markets; they attempt to predict taste and buying patterns, to satiate public demand with an identifiable range of products. And if you, the customer do not like what is on offer, there is no question of ordering something else.

By contrast, the bookseller's job of maintaining adequate stock (from the huge number of products on offer) and providing scope for the possible interests of the impulse buyer, yet tying up as little capital as possible, is a difficult balancing act.

Involvement in stock
Are booksellers merely storing titles for publishers or taking responsibility for trying to sell them?

> Publishers are the punters, they take the risks – booksellers don't.
> (Rivers Scott, literary agent interviewed in the *Sunday Telegraph*, 14 February 1993)

I remember, when the first branch of Waterstones opened, hearing how they had recruited sales staff who were enthusiastic about books, and how the shop stayed open until late at night. It sounded too good to be true. We have all experienced the power of recommendation at the point of sale and know how this can result in actual sales. During a student holiday job in Marks & Spencers I witnessed in-store competitions; different sections competed to suggest alternatives when the product the customer required was out of stock. Karen Geary (Marketing Director of Hamish Hamilton) testified to the power of recommendation during her time behind a till in the run-up to Christmas 1991.

Yet the suspicion often persists among publishers that too many book-sellers regard themselves as storing, rather than taking responsibility for, their stock. Publishers worry that June Formby's determination to run the shop (she is Manager of the Pan Bookshop, Fulham Road) 'as if it was mine and my last brass farthing was in it; it's the only way to run a bookshop' is not typical.

When it comes to defending books as value for money, it is surely no coincidence that the buck stops with the publisher rather than the book-seller. The sales director of a major quality trade publisher speculated that most booksellers, far from defending their wares, think that books are expensive. With a list full of Booker prize standard authors, she now has a standard letter on computer file defending the price of books. Why, she complains, are booksellers so uncommitted to their stock and their profession that they write to her enclosing a letter from a member of the public who thinks books are expensive, and ask her to explain. Lack of ultimate financial responsibility for the stock (in that they can be returned) surely either creates, or compounds, the problem.

Returns

The new distribution director of Faber and Faber had lots of experience in managing warehouses and organising carriers, but not much in books. The commodity he had previously managed, frozen chickens, once out of his warehouse, stayed out. Why, he asked, were books any different?

The bookseller's right to 'see-safe', or return ('de-stock' is the current term) items that he or she cannot sell, in return for a credit, underpinned the NBA; it ensured the public availability of a wide range of books. The concept was strengthened by contact with the magazine industry, where 'sale or return' is standard practice, when mass market publishers used magazine wholesalers and CTN outlets to distribute.

> The return is the most expensive part of bookshop life: capital intensive, labour intensive, and totally committed to money out – books that have already been paid for. Returns are a mark of a bookseller's level of competence, EPOS should be telling them what not to reorder.
>
> (David Whitaker, *Bookseller*, 29 March 1991)

But has the level of returns got out of hand? In the late summer of 1991 returns of mass market paperbacks from some shops were as high as 40 per cent. Returns have become a substantial determinant in publishers' profit forecasts; it is extremely difficult to judge how titles are selling in the high street and makes possible the nightmare scenario of reprinting a title just as the existing stock arrives back. Reps have always found it difficult to get new stock into shops before the previous season's returns have been authorised; in 1992 some larger booksellers no longer bothered with the formality of a signature.

The increase in returns of late has been substantial – Philip Kogan speculated around 20 per cent – probably at least as large as the drop in title sales. But is this increase a necessary evil as the book business gets bigger, reaching more and more outlets:

> the greater the attempt to maximise sales, the greater the risk of generating unsolds.
>
> (Paul Whitnall, Sceptre Books)

Or does the right to return block responsible buying by the retail trade?

Would they try harder to sell items they had committed themselves to, were their money indefinitely, as opposed to temporarily, tied up?

What do other industries do?

In most retail situations, buying is seen as a lasting commitment, hence, once recession hit, the boom in shops selling bankrupt stock. But there are exceptions such as paint, seeds and magazines, all of which are effectively rented to retail outlets, and the same rule applies when new merchandise, of which the store has no previous experience, is on offer. It is standard practice in supermarkets for stock for major new promotional incentives to be supplied on the basis of 'uplift' if it does not sell. Smaller independent stores, such as hardware shops or wine merchants, are occasionally offered promotional displays, for which the accompanying stock is available on sale or return, but I heard several complaints that most shops were just not big enough to accommodate the size of stand on offer.

Publishers, it has always been argued, need this flexibility to be able to persuade stockists to take books by unknown authors, or books for special promotions and one-off events such as author signing sessions. Even today, most publishers probably would not quibble at a right to make returns, but do resent the extent to which the facility is being used.

The scale and costs of the problem

It is certainly true that the number of titles publishers are producing compounds the problem, but the situation is undeniably more painful for publishers than booksellers.

When making returns the bookseller must pay only the direct and indirect (staffing, overheads and so on) costs of physically returning the books. Stock is returned for credit at full value, even if, as often happens, the books are no longer in saleable condition. Often, particularly for paperback publishers, the costs of separating re-usable from damaged is too high, and all returns are pulped.

The publisher, on the other hand, cannot send the stock back to the printer. Their internal profit account will be credited only with the manufacturer's cost of the stock (with a clawed back contribution from author royalties) while all the expenses of the previous sale (editorial, promotion, distribution, general overheads and so on) have to be written off. It is certainly true that the loss sustained by the publisher owing to each return significantly exceeds the profit on a book that sticks; probably by a factor of two to three. Distributors charge 10 – 13 per cent for their return service, at least double the publisher's profit margin.

So, what are the alternatives to returns?

Firm sale

The sense of a policy of firm sale sounds obvious. The reasons why it is not fully embraced highlight the slightly 'different' nature of the book trade.

There is a fear that firm sales will lead to smaller orders for fewer titles, and that subsequent paperback sales will be damaged by surplus hardback sales. This has happened in Australia, where firm sale at high bulk discounts has become quite prevalent on big bestsellers, and surplus copies are widely remaindered, affecting new title sales and paperback editions.

In the UK, Waterstones are currently experimenting with firm buying arrangements from seven general trade publishers. They gain extra discount in return for firm commitment but, if the titles do not sell during the initial shelf life in stores, must bear the costs of transporting them back to a central warehouse, and the fact that their capital is tied up until they are able to discount them in a sale.

The sense behind this move is undeniable, but the arrangement raises several questions. At what point will titles become eligible for marking down? The NBA, which Waterstones are determined not to break, says a year but there have been calls for a revised NBA which allows marking down after six months, under such buying arrangements. When books that do not sell through retail outlets are returned to the publisher, through sale or return, it is the publisher who makes the eventual decision on whether or not to reduce them in price and sell as remainder stock. If, on the other hand, the stock has been bought firm by the retailer, it is the retailer who takes the depreciation. And although the retailer must first offer the books back to the publisher before reducing the price, the impetus for reduction must necessarily come from them.

Jo Howard, Commercial Director of Waterstones, confirmed that storage facilities for stock bought firm were limited in many of their stores, and that the arrangements they have had to make for a central warehouse, as well as transportation costs, have to be offset against the margin. And even with firm sales, publishers still need to offer booksellers a degree of flexibility for individual promotions such as book signings.

The Society of Authors was also worried that firm sales would lead to a reduction in authors' royalties as shops would be unwilling to risk capital by stocking new authors. Shops will only buy firm in return for extra discount, and this disadvantages the author (in most contracts it says that over a certain discount the author will no longer receive the full royalty).

The need for tighter procedures

In trying to deal with the problem of returns, publishers arguably need to implement much greater financial control. They should, for example, try to establish maximum periods for returning overstocks and authorisation procedures and stick to them. Likewise, the real costs of supplying each account must be considered – is it profitable? It is also important, for their own financial survival, to continue with direct sales, which have a spin-off for the trade and which have few returns (usually only if the customer is dissatisfied with the product). And at the same time, of course, refraining from overselling and publishing fewer books would improve the situation.

Their difficult situation is amplified when large trade customers flout the rules. Simon Master of Random House commented to the *Bookseller* (19 June 1992) that Dillons were not the only people sending back returns, but:

> they are the only ones sending them back in this sort of volume in relation to our trade with them, and the only ones sending back unauthorised returns in significant numbers.

Similarly, delaying payment long beyond publishers' trading terms is becoming increasingly common, and this has severe effects on cash flow, in particular for smaller publishing houses. Is this the economics of the market-place or abuse of commercial power? I suspect that only in the book trade would we bother to ask such a question. Meanwhile, the larger publishing groups have improved cash collection by using effective credit management techniques.

There is also a growing consensus in the trade for some sort of penalisation for returns above a certain level. The wholesalers have already started. Bertrams introduced what amounts to a handling charge, and offer no returns on repeat orders. Gardners give a quarterly returns allowance of up to 5 per cent of a bookseller's total purchases in that period; other firms deal by negotiation.

More promotions

The best remedy all round is to increase demand; booksellers and publishers working together on both individual publisher and general industry promotions.

Dorling Kindersley have found more promotion leads to fewer returns. They spend over 12 per cent of turnover on promoting UK bookshop sales, and in 1991 returns amounted to less than 4 per cent of stock.

Size of order and discount offered

A manufacturer of fizzy drinks has one order for 2000 bottles, another for ten. Who gets the bigger discount and which order is fulfilled first? Can you honestly blame him?

In economic terms it seems sensible for any company to pay more attention to those customers who buy more, as Macmillan put it, to 'relate costs more closely to sales revenue'. And while it seems that small retailers of products other than books accept that their smaller orders receive lower discounts, and may attract postage and packing charges if under a certain threshold, small booksellers complain bitterly of the standard of service they receive compared with the larger players.

There are several reasons why publishers should consider subsidising operations, and 'price their product recognising that a certain proportion of sales will be uneconomic' (David Fussell, Colophon Bookshop, Wallingford).

(a) In the general interests of the wider availability of literature, the same principle that supports the NBA;

(b) To support the kind of customer service that breeds loyalty. Single copy orders (these three words seem to constitute a swear word at the BA conference) are often special orders, for which a cash deposit has been paid, the sort that independent booksellers will be determined to fulfil because they bring repeat business. 'We believe that the two most important factors in retailing are buying and customer service – the latter sometimes achieved almost at any price in order to secure a future customer' (Alex Bennett, the Amberstone Bookshop, Ipswich).

But they are undeniably expensive to fulfil. Selecting a single copy from a huge warehouse (admittedly mostly built in the 1960s and 1970s with higher trade volume in mind) is costly. A rough estimate suggests that the direct costs of selecting a single copy of a £15 hardback book are around £3. Tony Wagstaff, director of the distributor Biblios, estimated that the break-even point on distribution is reached when a consignment is valued at between £50 and £60, or when the distribution cost recovery is about £5. A previous PA survey suggested that up to 20 per cent of special customers' orders are supplied at a loss. Publishers consolidate orders and practise cyclical fulfilment ('picking' order from the shelves) to make the most cost-effective use of staff and carriers. (At the same time, they complain of a complete lack of order consolidation at the bookseller's end; for example, it is common for several different single copy orders to arrive from one bookseller to a publisher on the same day.)

(c) To support retail outlets of all sizes and help the whole market to grow. In America it is illegal to discriminate between small and large operations in terms offered, so publishers offer volume discounts with the booksellers paying carriage, thus benefiting the larger and more efficient stock-holding bookshops. In the UK, would all booksellers really

133

be willing to accept higher unit costs, reduced discounts and credit periods to pay for no single order surcharges on smaller customer orders? Why should the larger orderers do so? Would equal terms for all really enable smaller outfits to grow faster? Or is this just another cost (in addition to computerisation and returns already discussed) which the retail market is expecting the publishers to shoulder alone?

Booksellers complain that publishers are willing to provide single copies of books by direct marketing their customers, but there are distinct market differences in selling in this way. Publishers are usually selling high priced titles that bookshops do (or will) not stock, and the mailing costs are paid for out of the saved retailer margin; they sell at full price plus carriage at cost. At the same time they are building up a database of people, who find it more convenient to buy by post, to access in the future. And the selling of books by direct marketing is not an option restricted to publishers, as successful operations run by booksellers Wyvern Crest and Alan Armstrong have shown. Likewise, Quartet (Digital Care) has developed a specialised marketing and mailing system which uses data downloaded from Vista. And cumulatively, as has been repeatedly proved, these initiatives increase the market for books.

Speed of order processing and delivery

Industrial buyers accept that the shorter the lead time, the more you pay for the product. It is also standard practice for the length of delivery time to be established when the order is placed, and then built into the timing of the job. Carriage is normally the responsibility of the supplier, but may be switched if the goods are urgently required.

Booksellers may be frustrated that when asked by the customer 'when will it be here?', they cannot give a precise answer. It is natural for someone ordering anything (not just a book) to ask how long it will take to arrive. This does not mean that any wait at all is unsatisfactory. Should booksellers not be promoting their ability to order any one of the thousands of books in print in this country as a valuable customer service, rather than homing in on why the book in question cannot be there within 48 hours once the order is placed?

At the same time, wholesalers can provide a limited range of titles at 24 hours' notice, thereby enabling booksellers to use their services as an expanded stockroom. Should publishers be expected to do the same? Most publishers feel that the express provision of basic shop stock is unreasonable. Since nearly all titles are available 'see-safe' (ie they can be returned for a credit if they do not sell), booksellers should manage their stock requirements better and reorder with the publishers' systems in mind, not send in 'last-minute panic notes'.

For the well-managed shop, not all orders are required immediately. Desmond Clarke has speculated that for most bookshops there are three types of order with corresponding levels of need:

- general stock shop, for which a two-week turnaround is acceptable and can be built into booksellers' systems;
- special customer orders, available within a week;
- a premier service of short-term (48- or 72-hour) availability.

Obviously, the costs of fulfilling these different types of order vary considerably, and there is no point in paying for next-day delivery if it is not absolutely necessary. At the moment, the provision of titles 'carriage free' removes the responsibility of the bookseller deciding whether an order is urgent or just routine stock, and publishers' financial interests are not the top priority of most retail outlets.

Some publishers are now looking at the provision of differing distribution 'packages', depending on need – for example, 'carriage free' or 'carriage paid', a 48-hour guaranteed delivery at x per cent discount; a seven-day delivery at x + y per cent discount, similar to buying terms used in other industries. This would force booksellers to distinguish between rush and routine orders, balancing speed and cost with level of service required.

Booksellers complain of lost sales because of books in transit, but again, well-managed stock could help to alleviate this problem. In any case, the amount of stock missing because still on order does not seem to be enormous. The *Lost Sales* survey (see page 113) did not support booksellers' claims that much faster delivery times would increase sales significantly. It identified 4.1 per cent of total retail turnover as books not there because out of stock, and 2 per cent lost as they could not be found in the shop, even though they were there.

Reliability

Is speed of supply more important than reliability? Some booksellers complain that they have neither. Sue Butterworth of the Silver Moon Women's Bookshop commented that few publisher parcels can be unpacked and put on the shelves without checking the box contents first, but no other business that I have spoken to seemed to *expect* to be able to unpack without checking. Damaged stock, badly packed, is a frequent complaint, as are the redesigned-but-very-difficult-to-open cartons provided by some publishers who have tried to tackle the problem.

135

Payment period

Does the publisher require cheque with order, or is the bookseller being offered 30, 60 or 90 days' credit before payment is required?

The owner of a small gift shop I know in Kingston pays for everything by cheque, either handed to the delivery man or sent by return of post. This ensures that she receives first-class service from firms who supply her, on the same time schedule as Harrods and the major West End stores.

Other related issues

Possibilities for collective distribution arrangements

John Brown of *Viz* has several times made the case for a single industry-owned distribution centre, perhaps centred under just one or two industry-owned warehouses. A *Centraal Boekhuis* style operation would certainly be popular on the Continent. He cites as evidence for this the smooth news trade distribution:

> The advantage of the news trade is one delivery to one distributor: one invoice; full SOR [sale or return], but the whole print run is distributed immediately and the vast bulk of payment is received within two months of publication.
>
> (*Bookseller*, 25 May 1990)

Silver Moon too have suggested a joint industry wholesaling warehouse.

The disadvantage for the publisher is that titles are only distributed this way as long as they are selling; this is little help for the slow-moving backlist. Also the ever-reducing quantities that publishers claim they are able to sell would mean that the threshold for stocking would be low, and perhaps uneconomic. Arrangements would also be complicated by the sheer volume of different products available.

As usual there are frequent calls for the industry's organisations to coordinate, or at least investigate, other collective options. For example, could the BA look into a scheme for quantities of small bookshops to install teleordering at the same time and benefit from a discount (May 1991)? Would the BA and the PA like to look into the possibility of reviving a wholesaler dealing in specialist books, such as the now defunct Simpkin and Marshall (September 1990), or the viewing platform previously provided by SPEX before it grew into the London Book Fair and smaller houses could no longer afford to attend.

Distribution and customer service

Service is not something the British are very good at. We tend to regard it as rather demeaning, and wince at the notion of 'customer care' as being very American (and consequently unBritish), as well as irritatingly alliterative. The customer may in theory 'be king', but in practice is usually anything but.

But in difficult trading conditions such as a recession, good customer service is particularly important. Stores are often judged on the quality of their help, and that loyalty can prove important. For example, in the USA in 1991, at the height of the recession, the New York department store Bloomingdales made a commitment to improve service. They hired extra staff to shorten queues, opened a Federal Express desk to make it easier for customers to send goods out of town, and improved the gift-wrapping and collection facilities. The same goes for actual or impending competition: the ferry companies have improved dramatically of late and I am sure the threat from the Channel Tunnel is no coincidence.

Publishers too are sharpening up their act, improving their range of services to gain competitive advantage:

> It is the service and commitment to the end consumer which must become number one priority.
>
> (Terry Maher, *Bookseller*, 27 April 1990)

This is a far wider objective than just being nice to customers. Companies which try to improve their performance believe that improvement in service is measurable, and has a direct and beneficial spin-off. ITPS, for example, found that implementing a service programme, and the consequent better levels of satisfaction, resulted in much speedier cash collection. They also found that their publishers could sell 'distribution as a positive bargaining factor when negotiating terms of trade'.

Such companies also chart how they meet changing customer expectations and how they compare both with the performance of their publishing competitors and the service performance of other industries.

Performance is often tracked through survey. For example, at ITPS there has been extensive monitoring, through telephone surveys, meetings with small groups of major booksellers and random questionnairing (20,000 a year) of both account and individual customers on the service they received. Often customers report how surprised they are when reports of indifferent or poor performance are followed up and amends made.

This can be followed up with practical improvements, such as invoicing German customers in Deutschmarks, employing fluent French speakers to deal with Parisian customers, and having a proper understanding of local needs. In response to retail demand, Wiley tried opening their trade counter on Saturday mornings during the key academic period (not a success). Sheila O'Reilly, Customer Services Manager of Harcourt Brace Jovanovich, integrated credit control into the service department and arranged for regular meetings between credit control and sales staff. She invited booksellers to visit and arranged for sales and service staff to spend more time on the road with customers, in order to understand their problems better.

Even without embarking on surveying or restructuring, there is considerable room for improved service through changing attitudes, on both sides of the trade.

If it is true that:

> Independents usually bolster customer service in response to competition from the chains.
>
> (John Mutter, *Publishers Weekly* (US), 1 January 1992)

Booksellers could invest in more staff training, and lay more emphasis on the variety of services offered to the customer, such as ordering, title information, experience, advice, customer recognition – and enthusiasm, exactly the same benefits that other small retailers stress to encourage their customers to carry on using them rather than switching completely to the superstores. Some smaller booksellers are already finding that the 24-hour delivery service at normal trade terms (sometimes increased terms according to turnover), on offer to them from wholesalers, enables them to improve the service that they offer their customers:

> The old publisher/bookseller relationship becomes much less close, with some inherent dangers. But on the plus side, it becomes possible for the small independent to offer the sort of service that is undreamt of in other trades. If Waterstones' 'pile them high' is one way to sell extra books, knowledgeable advice backed up by 24-hour service is another.
>
> (Matthew Huntley, P and G Wells, Winchester)

Similarly, publishers should educate all staff in the importance of supplying accurate and up-to-date information to Whitaker's, and improve the liaison between their marketing and distribution departments.

Chapter 8

Who are the Book People?

> Publishers are usually not very intelligent, or they might be intelligent, but it's usually hard to tell.
>
> (Le Roi Jones, 1966)

This is one of those annoying remarks – after rereading it several times you still do not know whether you have been told something very profound or utterly meaningless.

What I detect is a feeling that because publishers carry on publishing, they must either be rather foolish (because they are too stupid to see any other options), or totally immersed in what they are doing (and hence to be envied for a fascinating vocation). Both explanations highlight something 'different' about the book trade, and I plan to explore aspects of publisher character and motivation in this chapter, considering who works in the industry, why, and how long they stay.

The people who make up the industry *are* important. I have already looked in Chapters 1 and 4 at how publishing is a people-centred business, at the importance of flair, hunch and contacts:

> Publishing remains an intensely people-orientated business and it always will. It is a business of taste and choice.
>
> (Trevor Glover, Penguin)

What kind of people make good publishers, and in what kind of operation do they best thrive?

A recent survey of the Society of Young Publishers (SYP) showed that 90 per cent of its membership were from professional middle-class families. They were also well educated, 80 per cent having been in higher education. As one publishing course lecturer put it, there are far more enrolments on to publishing courses from Carolines than Kylies. Potential publishers tend to be highly articulate, confident and independent. They

139

are also predominantly female – West Herts College cited an 80 – 20 per cent split in both their enquiries and enrolments, and this pattern is confirmed in other colleges, and in other countries. In Europe too publishing has cachet and attracts well-motivated candidates. In the USA publishers are predominantly white, middle class, educated, and from the East Coast.

Publishers are single-minded about their chosen career. Whereas most of the final-year degree students of my acquaintance chose a particular job function (for example, to be an accountant or go into management), few laid down precisely which industry they wanted to work in. Publishers, it seems here, really are different.

For instance, those who wanted to work as a buyer had to find a firm willing to employ and train them as such. The ease with which this could be achieved depended on the economy and the number of jobs on offer, but if one firm turned them down there were others to be considered. Application was relatively straightforward: they filled in the relevant form, sent it to the right building, and then hoped for an interview. Sometimes they would try several buildings in a short space of time.

By contrast, the first task of those interested in a career in publishing was to carry out detailed planning as to where the most appropriate buildings were. They then progressed to charting who they already knew inside them, and circumnavigated them to find the back door, the fire escape or any ladders left casually lying about. Formal application forms for specific job opportunities were rare. There were few company brochures to read about relevant products; it was a question of picking a few names you had heard of and scanning the shelves of the local bookshop for more information about the kind of books produced. Applicants had to be enthusiastic, enterprising, optimistic and determined.

Above all, anyone decided on a career in publishing had to leave their options open until the last minute. Most job application forms for the higher education leaver 'milk round' are filled in six to nine months before finals, with a starting date of the following September. Most publishing vacancies are only advertised a month or more before the successful candidate is needed to start, so there are few future publishers with a pre-exam job offer.

Careers advisers tell me that the general job application market has, of late, moved in a similar way to publishing. Moving to London and taking a secretarial course, or dusting the warehouse shelves during your university holidays, has always been an accepted way to make contacts, acquire industry knowledge and then get into publishing. Today there is much more emphasis on the indirect approach in other professions too, on the 'added value' that individual applicants are able to give to their curriculum vitae through related work experience and the acquisition of relevant skills.

Those offering professional career advice now include the 'indirect' or 'speculative approach' in their general guidance. For example, most of the graduates in the UK in 1992 who entered the Diplomatic Service had done something 'additional' first; few entered straight from university. And this emphasis on self-organised, pre-job training, is the way that the employment market has operated in continental Europe and the USA for some time.

Why publishing?

The SYP survey showed that nearly all the 300 members quoted had joined publishing because of a 'love of books' and, despite the 'appallingly low' wages, 92 per cent were planning to stay. Ivor Powell of West Herts College commented on the relish with which most potential publishers long to be part of the 'book-producing community', creating a quality product that matters. Many had family connections. And once they have found a niche within publishing, few move outside the industry. It is a more common career path to work for a few firms and then set up on your own than to change industry.

> Almost all the people in charge of the large British companies are from the publishing world. We are not businessmen or women who happen to be in publishing. We are publishers who have learned about business.
> (Trevor Glover, Managing Director of Penguin UK, *Bookseller*, 16 August 1991)

And it seems that the same goes throughout Europe and the USA. Publishing is a congenial place to work and it is hard to get started. It follows that those who make it are motivated and determined.

An introspective environment

Appointments from outside the industry are few. There have been experiments but they are remarkable rather than usual. Astron commented that most publishers feel more comfortable appointing either other publishers or complete beginners. Alan Hill commented that he has 'always preferred someone new to the game, but with first-class potential, to a second rater with experience' and by taking on new graduates he earned spectacular loyalty, as evinced by the time most of them stayed working for him. Publishers find it hard to understand the motivation of those who have left the industry and then desire to come back in. And low pay does not attract many who have no previous experience of the book trade.

There are exceptions. Derek Searle arrived to work at Transworld as Sales Director in 1979 with a background in advertising and fast-moving consumer goods. With a literary degree, and a lifelong love of reading and books, he considered a move to publishing a natural one. What seemed less natural was the time it took to appoint him (five interviews with the same company) and, once within the industry, the time he found it took to make decisions. In the world outside publishing, he told me, the decision to produce a particular product is based on the scientific application of marketing principles: market research reveals who has the need and is likely to be interested; market profiles tell you how to reach them and how they like to buy. In publishing he found a complete contrast: market research was little used, and there was far more reliance on persuasive argument supported by hunch – and endless meetings to discuss!

Alan Wherry left school with A levels, and worked in the fast-moving consumer goods industry for 14 years, ending up with Procter and Gamble, before deciding that it was possible to do something you liked for a living. He found making the transition to publishing much easier than everyone outside the industry seemed to think possible. (He believes that no one in publishing *has* found it particularly difficult to get in; it's a rumour put around by those who were put off before they even tried.)

He arrived, like any other new recruit to publishing, with a love of books. But with a non-publishing background and immediate installation at director level, he did understand that existing staff felt threatened. It did not worry him unduly. The particular skill he felt he was able to offer was that of good management, a skill he found sadly lacking in the industry.

Having started as Sales Director of Corgi, he subsequently moved on to Penguin, and then became one of the founder directors of Bloomsbury. He says that the great joy of publishing, and the one he plans to stay for, is the immensely flexible nature of the industry. The essential quality of a good publisher is that of entrepreneur and opportunity spotter, and at Bloomsbury he has been able to combine different roles to this end, which together provide immense job satisfaction. Although Sales and Marketing Director, he also commissions (Bloomsbury have published several books found by him) and travels a good deal.

Believing that the book industry today still lacks good management ('it's the publishing malaise'), at Bloomsbury he places great importance on training and management education, to help people understand their job functions and so come up with better ways of performing. He feels that in the past publishers have relied too much on the way things have always been done. If publishers are loath to recruit from outside their industry, they seem to be equally slow to see the merits of those from within who have slightly different experience from their own. 'Books are different' seems to subdivide neatly into sects who believe that 'trade/educational/academic books are different'.

Sales representatives or distribution executives who took their jobs in order to advance into mainstream publishing find it difficult to do so (although being an export rep seems to have sufficient kudos to avoid this trap). Even proven editorial skills may be deemed unsuitable if the market to be approached is not exactly the same. Many firms have traditionally hostile relations between editorial and sales departments, and rights are usually a one-way street. (Felicity Rubenstein's advancement from that department to be Managing Director of Macmillan London was unusual, but it is worth noting that the process started through personal contact rather than formal job application.)

And great snobbism persists. Alan Giles, the WH Smith highflyer, appointed by the group to take over as Managing Director of Waterstones from February 1993, was described dismissively by the *Guardian* as 'the man from Do It All', and speculation continues as to how 'bookish' he really is (by his own admission, not very, but how important is that?).

Most publishers are conscious that they work for lower wages than their contemporaries in other industries:

> It used to be true that the only two ventures people entered for love rather than money were to own a football club and to own a publishing house.

> (Alan Giles, WH Smith)

And some of the profit levels recorded by publishing houses in recent years confirm that their owners would have done better to stick their money in a building society!

But although many publishers would certainly earn more selling toothpaste or washing powder, they do not want to; they thrive on the product variety that publishing offers. Paul Scherer admitted that he returned to mainstream publishing because he missed diversity in Mills and Boon's single product world. Publishers also believe in their own product superiority. John Brown's boast that he does not share the passion of his colleagues for books, and that he would be 'just as happy selling records' is not common. Many would sympathise with Peter Owen's conviction that: 'I won't do bad books on the whole, because if I were going to do that I might as well have done something else, like being in the grocery business.' And an equally passionate commitment to the business of literacy and reading can be found in bookshops, in particular the small independent kind. Several booksellers I spoke to talked with great enthusiasm of the enormous satisfaction of matching customer and reading material, marred only by their frustration with ever-rising overheads.

The industry is too, in the main, a civilised place to work:

> The nature of the book trade is that it is extremely clubbable, and it has the rather appealing characteristic that people see each other and behave with courtesy to each other. (It is not true of all industries. Aluminium smelters regard each other with suspicion.)
>
> (Eric de Bellaigue, *Bookseller*, 7 June 1991)

But civilisation does not mean that professional marketing techniques are irrelevant. There is a world of difference between pushing cocaine and cornflakes, and many influential figures in the industry, such as Richard Charkin and Julian Rivers, now speak openly of the buzz they get from doing big deals and gaining market share. For example, Charkin's Damascus-like experience was selling the *Oxford Books of Flowers, Birds* and *Seashells* to Hamlyn; they went from selling 500 to 40,000 copies a year. Listening to them it would be hard not to be affected by their enthusiasm.

It is also too easy for this love of books to spill over into xenophobia for anyone who works on any other kind of product; the dangerous result can be that books are consequently promoted as élitist individual purchases rather than mainstream necessities. Many feel this still happens; Pete Ayrton of Serpent's Tail criticised:

> the elitism of the [Oxbridge] culture that directs publishing in this country – a coterie of like-minded people who decide what will be published and in what form.
>
> (*Bookseller*, 1 May 1992)

> It's not about nice young things anymore, but there is still a long way to go. It's a very traditional industry.
>
> (Andrew Welham, interview with *Marketing Week*, 12 July 1991)

Publishers certainly get away with a few trade practices that are rather dubious. For example, it is common practice to accept orders and money from the public for books not yet published, and then, if the books are delayed, to hold on to that money without interest until they are. The Mail Order Protection Scheme lays down that all goods advertised through the post should be available and supplied within 28 days. Similarly, trade information pieces to suppliers frequently quote prices that are subsequently changed; invoices for orders received go out without warning of the higher price. (Most retailers accept that, given the low price of books, the margin of error does not, in most cases, make it cost effective to inform everyone of raised prices. What they do resent is the frequency with which this happens.)

There are signs that things are tightening up a bit, and that the authorities are more ready to intervene. The European Court recently ruled on the NBA and, rather ironically, given the PA's stance on the protection of copyright, HarperCollins were fined for misleading buyers by presenting Alistair MacLean plots by Alastair MacNeill, in charges brought by Warwickshire trading standards department.

What publishers are paid

Publishing is traditionally seen as a low pay industry, as indeed are many other attractive jobs for which the entry is similarly competitive; for example, working in the broadcast media, in a museum or art gallery or for a fine wine company. Most graduates probably start work on around £10,000 outside London, £12,000 in the capital. But this starter level of pay is absolutely in line with what other industries are offering, now that the ludicrously high initial salaries on offer in the City a few years ago have fallen and manufacturing firms too have not increased their offers greatly of late. In 1992 a 21-year-old graduate with a second-class degree received an average starting salary of £12,800, a 2.4 per cent increase on the 1991 rate.

Low levels of pay in publishing start to appear more pronounced after a few years' experience in the industry. The SYP survey showed that with an average members' age of 28, average earnings were £13,700, which the society described as 'appallingly low'. One graduate female editor was earning only £10,000 a year before tax.

Higher up, the best way to increase your salary is to move job. But even for management, wages seem to be a good 20 – 30 per cent below equivalent jobs outside the industry. MBAs occasionally make contact with Astron, but the level of pay on offer generally makes them look elsewhere. There is, however, a tendency in the industry to pay more for transferable skills, such as accountancy, or in departments of publishing houses where there is a measurable link between individual effort and resulting sales, such as direct marketing. In other areas of publishing, for example, the publications departments of non-publishing companies, or what Rosemary Roberts of Oxford Brookes University called 'the sharp end of information technology in the industry', wages can be much higher.

Even so, few publishers are planning to leave the industry; job satisfaction and fascination count for much, and it is still seen from outside as a high-status industry. Richard Charkin commented after a three-month course at Harvard, during which he mixed with senior managers from all sorts of industrial sectors, that he was the poorest person there, but the one with the highest level of job satisfaction. He reckoned that 50 per cent of the course envied him his job.

Career patterns in publishing

Once it was believed that to succeed it was necessary to have worked in four different companies by the time a publisher was in his or her 30s.

(David Whitaker)

Today the trend seems to be for less company-hopping. In part this is the result of the recession, which makes employees less willing to risk a career move. But the larger groups of publishers are increasingly able to offer different job experiences without requiring the employee to leave in search of such variety. Larger corporations endeavour to keep key people longer, leading perhaps, in the long term, to a decline in quality. David Whitaker claimed he has seen 'too many publishers who I believe have been shrunk by corporatism'. Philip Joseph, Chairman of Books Etc, lamented the decline of the fanatic: 'awful people to work with, but without them things just don't work.'

Certainly, my own experience, of both working for 'fanatics' and in running training courses at Book House, has tended to show that prolonged corporation can breed an unexciting mind, an unwillingness to find out how the implications of one person's actions affect others (usually because they come under the orbit of a different department), a reluctance to experiment or think laterally. And while no one would wish redundancy on a colleague, Bob Osborne of Butterworth-Heinemann pointed out that, when it happens to you, it can undeniably have a positive effect, making you reconsider values you never questioned before. (How does my area of work fit with the company's main priorities? How much money do I bring in towards paying my salary?) These are the questions that any new freelance must consider: tidying one's desk is not invoicable.

Large or small firm? What is the best working environment for publishers?

I have already talked about the polarisation of the retail end of the trade, whether there is much common ground between those who have used the last ten years to open chains of shops and those who have stayed put, but continue to write articulate letters to the *Bookseller* about high prices and single order surcharges. It is interesting, in this context, to look at the importance of company size in publishing, to see if small implies dynamic or inefficient, and large stable or sluggish. The only constant over the past few years has been change, and the diversity that now exists says something interesting about the nature of publishing.

The late 1980s and early 1990s saw some massive conglomerates emerge: Collins went to Murdoch and Octopus to Reed. Anthony Cheetham bough Hutchinson, CVBC bought the union, and the firm that eventually emerged was Random Century. All these 'marriages' were seeking the stability of funding that comes from belonging to a large group, preferably not reliant on one industrial sector alone. They were also after 'economies of scale'. Both motives arose largely from the difficulties of recession.

There were some reports of ideal marriages, supportive owners backing dynamic management but supplying much necessary funding. For example, both Graham and Trotman and Stanley Thornes speak highly of Kluwer, and Transworld of Bertelsmann. But in general, the most powerful message that has emerged from these unions is that strategic rationale for merger is vital: size alone does not bring either efficiency or saving.

> Size is not necessarily an advantage ... there's a natural tendency within publishing for smaller units to flourish, and that the conglomeration of publishing units is a rather unnatural tendency.
>
> (Eric de Bellaigue, 7 June 1991)

Conglomerates are not famous for their ability to keep overheads down. Indeed, the advances war that money from these unions arguably funded was at times quite irrational.

Similarly, the grouping of diverse interests often brought no cost reductions at all; ramshackle interests are expensive to manage. For example, the ownership of several different lists may still require different rep forces to subscribe them, if each list sells to a different kind of outlet. And the major expenses of any publishing house are not subject, or are subject to only very small, economies of scale: you can't buy authorship or print much cheaper in quantity. It is difficult to predict the critical mass at which union is necessary, but Tim Hely Hutchinson tried to put a figure on it:

> there are no economies of scale to be had in trade publishing beyond sales of about £3 million, possibly less.
>
> (*Bookseller*, 6 September 1991)

There followed some dramatic 'unbundlings'; entrepreneurial groups of individuals buying themselves out of larger corporations and starting again. Headline was started by Tim Hely Hutchinson, Sue Fletcher and Sian Thomas, all ex-Macdonald. Weidenfeld bought Dent; both were subsequently bought by Anthony Cheetham, newly ousted from what was renamed Random House. Some purchases or mergers were subsequently reversed by management buy-outs. For example, Julia MacRae and Nick Hern both left Walker Books; Christopher Sinclair Stevenson escaped from the Penguin Group, with his author list largely intact, only to be swallowed up later by Reed. One freelance I spoke to said that publishers could no longer afford the luxury of telling their senior management just what they thought of them before they left a job – they were too likely to find themselves under the same corporate umbrella again before too long!

The fall-out from some of these mergers was some very senior and talented people. As amalgamations had meant that there were fewer positions at the apexes of pyramids, several of them subsequently decided that if the corporate phase of their career was over, there were successful niches to be carved out as industry specialists and management consultants. For example, Paul Richardson (ex-Heinemann, Macmillan and Octopus) is now a successful consultant, mainly specialising in advising publishing companies in Eastern Europe, both on how to organise themselves and how to export their products. Richard Balkwill, former Editorial Director of Macmillan Education, is well established as an educational and copyright consultant and does a lot of training.

Other senior people have voluntarily opted out of the corporate environment and thereafter maintained a more 'hands-on' role. John Jackman, former Managing Director of Macmillan Education and Macmillan Children's Books, had always planned a move out of corporatism before the age of 50. His opportunity came when Macmillan sold off part of his responsibilities to Nelson. Today he runs a one-man publishing operation. He spends most of his time on large-scale packaging projects, although he still produces part of Macmillan's further education list and also offers management consultancy within the industry. Hamish MacGibbon, former Managing Director of Heinemann Educational Books and later Collins Educational now runs a three-man publishing company (supported by extensive use of freelance help), specialising in commissioned histories of businesses, schools and other institutions. Richard Mabb, WH Smith's book promotions manager, left the large corporation and set up an independent marketing and promotions service for publishers and wholesalers.

Many of these people have told me that, once established as an independent, consultancy work came relatively quickly. Most are now in the position of turning down jobs on the grounds of insufficient time or preference. Yet advice to the newly released in other industries lays a lot of emphasis on *not* assuming that you can just set up as a consultant in the industry you have left. There are probably several reasons why it is easier to become established as an independent in the book world.

The independent tradition

The publishing community is much larger than those employed by companies; most firms have an established tradition of using external people. Whereas in many other industries, outsiders are mostly used on an *ad hoc* basis, supplied by agencies on temporary contracts and, for the most part, at low levels of responsibility, publishing has always relied on experienced people working at home.

Given that publishing as an industry depends so heavily on taste and choice, differing viewpoints are highly valid.

> Unlike most manufacturing industries that deal with inanimate material, at the heart of publishing there is a human, personal and creative dimension that can never be ignored.

(Michael Sissons in an interview with the *Independent*, 24 January 1991)

Most publishing firms have long employed readers to give an opinion on manuscript submissions, and this can be a role of great significance. (Cape's rejection of Barbara Pym mid-career was as the result of reports by independent readers on her latest novel, on which the in-house staff relied. Tom Maschler subsequently said he regretted not having read the title in question himself.) Likewise, editorial and design services are often bought in rather than maintained full time in-house. Frank Delaney speculated that the buying-in of talent will have to happen more and more in the future:

> The old principle of reducing overheads has become almost the new gospel. Flair can often thrive better out of house. Industry that depends on the power of individual creation will increasingly need to buy in panache.

(Frank Delaney, *Bookseller*, 27 September 1991)

This has tended to mean that, within an industry still so reliant on contacts, people are respected for their depth of experience rather than their current corporate responsibilities. John Jackman commented that having decided to resign his senior corporate position, he offered his resignation to the Kettner Group, a meeting place for senior management in educational publishing companies (and the forerunner of the Educational Publishers Council). He was strongly urged to stay on; his experience was considered much more important than his current managerial head-count.

For those from other industrial sectors, without the same tradition of respect for, and use of, independent individuals, setting up on your own can be much harder. For example, those made redundant from City jobs have often found it difficult to set up as independent investment advisers – FIMBRA membership conditions, government restrictions on impartiality and independent advice through the Financial Services Act, and the effects of EC legislation, all conspire against the development of a freelance culture. Meanwhile, increasing competition and automation mean that only the select few get jobs in the same sector again.

The entrepreneurial streak

Good publishers are entrepreneurs, opportunity spotters, anticipators of taste:

> Publishing is supremely an entrepreneurial occupation: personal initiative is everything and motivation is the most precious quality.
> (Alan Hill, *In Pursuit of Publishing*, John Murray 1988)

And parts of the industry have often, in the past, sailed close to the wind – the margin between success and failure can be very small. This has tended to mean that there is sympathy, indeed empathy, with those who opt out – whether voluntarily or compulsorily – from the corporate scene. Reports have come back from those in other industries who, once made redundant, find themselves effectively ostracised. Perhaps there is a fear that bad luck will be catching, or that keeping in touch with those dismissed shows a preference for the company of losers. Or is publishing less status bound?

The lack of middle management in many large companies

The cuts made in many publishing companies have left a dearth of middle management talent. Several independent consultants commented that they had been asked to take part in the making of highly sensitive policy decisions, or involved in key company structures such as the setting up of new departments and the recruiting of important personnel – all areas that one might have expected to be the province of in-house personnel.

A little earlier in the career, redundancy has a similarly distressing effect, but does not seem to make all those affected head straight out of the industry (although being younger in the profession, arguably their options to do so are more open).

Hazel Hutchison was made redundant from her job as Sales and Marketing Manager for a general trade publisher in a sudden interview one morning, but was offered no reason for her dismissal from a job for which she had been head-hunted. She asked for a written reason, and half an hour later was offered 'we no longer require your services because of your attitude towards your job' together with a cardboard box so that her desk could be cleared immediately. Her successor escorted her from the building shortly afterwards. Yet despite this depressing experience, after nine years in the book trade, she desired to remain within it. She did go for interviews for product manager-type jobs in other industries, which were in general paying around £5000 – £10,000 more in salary than publishing houses to someone of her experience.

Her desire to stay within the trade became more determined as her unemployment progressed – the book-producing community were extremely sympathetic and supportive. She had many offers of freelance work, not all at her level, but they helped to pay the mortgage. And when she did land a full-time job, the response from former work contacts, who after her sudden departure had no idea where she had gone, was touching. She is now on the Women in Publishing committee, and of late several other members have found themselves out of work, and had similar experiences. Publishers in general seem to be good at supporting each other.

And those who (whether through choice or circumstances) decide to remain in freelance work do find that there is room in the industry for people offering basic services (for example, editorial, marketing, copywriting and so on) to make a living. Publishers have of late benefited, in that the number of people available, and the fact that many are looking for full-time employment, mean that they can insist on higher standards than was traditionally the case.

Some publishers now rely entirely on the freelance pool of trained staff, released on to the market through redundancy. Such firms can, for example, run large numbers of freelance editors, monitored by an overall managing editor, and benefit from the training provided by other companies without providing any of their own. Professional trainers argue that they are evading a moral responsibility: the other view is that they are providing much needed employment to people without full-time jobs, either through bad luck or choice.

The main medium for freelance work is still largely personal recommendation, although qualifications may become more important in the future. Freelancers are able to register to work towards a National Vocational Qualification (NVQ) at a special low rate subsidised by the Paul Hamlyn Foundation, and the early signs are that this will be popular.

The ranks of freelance designers too have been swelled by many publishers making the decision to buy in design services when needed, rather than keep them in-house full time. Costs for freelance design work can nevertheless be high compared with freelance editorial and publicity work, and often produce a determination to manage *without* design services as often as possible, using the printer, or someone in-house with 'an eye'.

The independent sector of publishing

The independent sector of publishing continues – not all the independent publishers have been swallowed up, despite offers. The Independent Publishers Guild has 290 members and, although this has fallen from a high of around 400 members a few years ago, the Secretary assured me that it is not the case that the entire balance have gone into larger unions or receivership.

Publishing has always been an industry where people can get started on their own quickly and cheaply; it is a lot more expensive to set up as a one-person welding operation than a one-person publishing company. One major book retailing chain told me that they receive announcements from at least a couple of new publishers every day, and that they find the costs of dealing with many small accounts extremely expensive.

Business origins in back bedrooms, like Sebastian Walker and Jessica Kingsley, are relatively common, although with the growth of the venture capital industry and the availability of equity investment capital to entrepreneurs from the mid-1980s, new companies were able to grow much more quickly than was traditionally possible. Headline was started in 1986 and Bloomsbury in 1987; both have since been launched on the stock market.

Independent firms such as Headline, Orion, John Murray, Faber and Souvenir are able to respond to the market quickly and to control costs, exploring specific niche markets in which the large corporations are not interested. While publication of a bestseller might be a disaster for a very small operation (it over-extends supply lines), they can often respond to the market much more quickly than large companies and meet real needs. Indeed, they can frequently specialise in producing the right kind of books for the kind of difficult trading conditions we are seeing at the moment:

> What does sell well in a recession is any decent self-help informational book, from gardening to cookery.
>
> (Graham Lord, *Daily Telegraph*, 4 January 1993)

The advantages that they are able to offer authors are particularly valuable in time of recession too, when job stability, and hence permanence of contacts, is difficult. They can provide a much more personal service and, crucially, supply belief at an early stage in the writer's career, from which both author and publisher reap long-term rewards.

> We prefer to build up our own list of the writers of the future rather than pay excessive sums for other people's authors.
>
> (Liz Calder, Bloomsbury, quoted in the *Guardian*, 20 March 1991)

Faber's Robert McCrum searches for nascent talent that they can publish from the beginning: Ishiguro's progress from first novel to Whitbread and Booker prize winner has proved the worthwhile nature of the long-term investment. Peter Owen, another independent publisher, paid an advance of £25 to Hermann Hesse for *Siddartha*. Fifteen years later, still published by Owen, he has grown to become one of the world's most fashionable authors. Owen has published eight Nobel prize winners and comments that: 'I have often found that a really good writer will eventually become profitable.'

Some independent firms have used the recession to regain control of parts of their company, previously sold to external investors. For example, Kogan Page bought back complete control by buying out Lazards, a minority investor. Independent firms within London and other major centres have also benefited from the fall-out of experienced staff, whom larger corporations are unwilling to employ as too expensive or, perhaps, too experienced for comfort. Kogan Page secured the services of Hamish MacGibbon as a non-executive director and the Independent Publishers Guild has as its president Tim Rix, the former Chairman and Chief Executive of one of Britain's largest publishers, the Longman Group.

So, regarding publisher size, the conclusion must be that there is no 'right' structure for a publisher to live in. The industry places vital importance on dynamism and ideas, and different solutions may provide the necessary background set-up.

Training in publishing

Level of training on arrival in the industry

Traditionally, publishers were trained 'on the job'. Recruits were usually graduates, but they started their working life in a junior capacity, perhaps as a secretary, or as an editorial or production assistant. In time, the new recruit took over the manager's job and the cycle started again.

Most new publishers still enter the industry at degree level. But just as the universities have experienced applicants' preference for more vocational courses in recent years, so we have also seen the emergence of publishing courses, offering specialist training with either degree courses or postgraduate diplomas. There are now ten such colleges offering publishing, often in combination with other fields of study such as cartography, psychology and computing. All the colleges try, with varying degrees of success, to ensure work experience as part of the course.

In practice, both work experience placements in industry, and people in industry willing to give their time to advise on course content and development, have been more difficult to find of late, and it is not difficult to understand why in a recession. But while individual colleges have built valuable links with industry (eg the Paul Hamlyn Foundation linking West Herts College with Longman and Oxford Brookes University with Butterworth-Heinemann), collective contact between those running these courses and the industry they train for, has been slow. It took Book House Training Centre to organise the first get-together between publishing personnel managers responsible for recruiting and those training students for such an opportunity.

In a traditional industry, the advocates of these courses are fighting an uphill battle: respect for the straight-subject degree from the 'blue chip' university is long established. Graduate recruitment schemes from the major groups seldom seem to look outside Oxford or Cambridge, probably because those doing the interviewing feel more comfortable with the product of their own Alma Mater. A few managers said they were suspicious of loose, 'over-arty' degrees offered by the newer universities, and there were comments about how publishing courses were too much concerned with the history of the industry and not enough with financial and managerial aspects (although it was hard to relate such prejudices to firsthand knowledge of course content!).

And it remains true that of the 200 publishing graduates each year, at least 40 – 50 per cent never enter the industry that they have trained to work in. They may end up using the skills learnt in related jobs – perhaps producing customer information for banks and building societies or inhouse journals for individual companies, all of which are publishing jobs – or go into related fields such as arts administration, public relations or advertising.

For some this is because other parts of a degree course studied along with publishing appeal more; others are lured away by undeniably higher wages. Other reasons for wanting to head straight out include better career progression (career paths in publishing can seem tortuous or at best overgrown); earlier responsibility; more interesting work from the outset, rather than having to earn your spurs on the dross. External organisations can frequently predict a more concrete long-term career plan and be able to offer definite vacancies three months ahead of finals when students are looking for jobs, not just at the last minute.

But there are signs that the merits of the new publishing courses, and the sound skills of those they turn out, are gradually being recognised:

> I feel, too, that the existence of courses such as this one and the skills and knowledge that they confer on students are gradually being recognised by publishers ... a number of publishers have written to us

during the year to advertise posts suitable for recent graduates ... a good sign.

(Rosemary Roberts, Principal Lecturer in Publishing, Oxford Brookes University)

All the course managers I spoke to attempt to keep in touch with graduates and find that they progress well and rapidly. If this positive record can be tied to actual cooperation between the colleges producing the recruits and the industry employing them, their collective reputation may grow further.

On-the-job training

Professional, on-the-job training has changed its image in recent years. It is now increasingly seen as a resource for promoting company profitability rather than an optional, if altruistic, luxury, which could be cut when times were hard.

Training is now more often viewed as a long-term, measurable benefit. Firms which offer appraisal, training courses and individual career progression generally get better value from, and retain, their staff for longer periods, and there is an undisputed correlation between those companies which invest in training and those which are successful. Angela Mansell, Longman's Director, Human Resources (Publishing), told me that they spend 2 per cent of the total payroll on training their staff, and this does not reveal the cost of all the in-house training provided by senior employees. Longman believe that this not only breeds loyalty and professionalism among their staff, but is a positive bargaining position when recruiting new employees.

This view has probably been supported by a growing awareness of population decline and the resulting shortage of potential management in years to come; hence the need for a better trained workforce all round. And for once there seems to be complete unanimity among the political parties about the need for professional training – there was a tri-party welcome to the development of NVQs. In 1992 Book House established the Publications Qualifications Board and is receiving applications from both full-time and freelance employees within the industry who want to work for a publishing NVQ. For the well-run company, this is a cost-effective form of monitoring training which is going on in any case. Requests for NVQ-qualified applicants are starting to appear in publishing job advertisements.

There are several examples that prove the existence of a developing training consciousness in publishing, in line with other industries.

155

– The increasing number of specialist firms offering dedicated publisher training – several run by ex-industry members – that continue to survive the recession.

Book House Training Centre has expanded its premises (supported in part by the Unwin Foundation Charitable Trust) and is training more people, on more courses than ever before. In 1990 BHTC trained 2300 people from 300 companies. Considering the recession, bookings have held up well during the last couple of years. The Courses Manager, Jean Hindmarch, reported that before booking firms are making detailed judgements about whether course contents will precisely meet their training needs. BHTC has also expanded in Ireland and Scotland.

Similarly, the expansion of the training side of Women in Publishing bears witness to continued interest in improving skills. Ten years ago WIP began offering their own training courses, run by their members and contacts, to help other women who wanted to get on in their careers. This need survives, but the range of courses on offer has expanded greatly and they now have a two-tier payment structure so that firms which can – and do – send delegates, pay more. And there are other specialist firms such as the Oxford Publicity Partnership offering publishing courses.

The BA too is promoting training to its members – it runs the Certificate in Bookselling Skills. It is, however, hampered by the fact that while the larger retailing groups can run their own courses, the owners of smaller firms are often too busy running their businesses to spare the time or cash, however acutely they recognise the need for training. A suspicion persists that once trained, staff will move on.

– The growth of a specialist literature and accompanying vocabulary ('human resource development'; 'total quality management'; 'quality circles' and so on). This has crept into publishing houses; for example, Judy Little is Longman's Human Resources Director, and the firm keeps up high-profile involvement in this area.

– The development of, and respect for, appraisal systems in industry and their implementation in many publishing firms.

Higher management training

The promotion of staff (with little direct management experience) to departmental management positions is common.

(Giles Clark, *Inside Book Publishing*, Blueprint 1988)

But there does seem to be an increasing value placed on management training in publishing today, backed, one suspects, by both the wider availability, and glamour, of the MBA in industry in general. Likewise, there is a greater respect for numeracy in publishing; accountants are running companies both efficiently and creatively (for example, David Heatherwick is joint Managing Director at Walker).

Courses are being offered at higher levels (by both Book House and the independent trainers) and more people are studying for them in their spare, or the company's, time. David Taylor at Blackwells is doing a company-sponsored part-time MBA; both Richard Charkin and Alan Giles went to the Harvard Business School (other companies may use spells at their US office to achieve a similar 'sharpening' effect for key employees). Longman is sponsoring employees through both full- and part-time MBAs, and although the facility was at first seen as an option for senior management, it is now down to the departmental training budgets of individual line managers to fund individuals who wish to take up the offer.

Comparison with publishing in other countries

One of the publicised benefits of an NVQ is that subsequent owners can take them into Europe – they are transferable and internationally recognised qualifications. But the Continent is already better trained, through two-way, contractual, arrangements.

For example, in Germany most new recruits to the book trade, whether to a publishing house or bookshop, enter a three-year apprenticeship organised through a system of *duales Ausbildungssystem* (dual training system). This scheme combines day release to *Berufschule* and on-the-job training at the sponsoring firm but, although the two forms of training work hand in hand, they are separate. The *Berufschule* is subordinate to the Ministry of Education, and final exams are taken before the *Industrie und Handelskammer*, an organisation which represents the interests of the employers and wants to improve the regional economy. As an alternative to weekly day release, the apprentice can opt for a three-month course at the *Buchhandlerschule* in Frankfurt, a private training organisation run by the *Börsenverein* – the federation of booksellers, publishers and wholesalers.

Once the apprenticeship has been completed (and there are few dropouts), few transfer to another industry. Some of the more promising newly qualified will progress to take a vocationally based degree (Mainz, Munich, Leipzig, Stuttgart and several other universities offer publishing in combination with other subjects) and so return to the industry with even stronger professional credentials. There is a similar system in the Netherlands through the Academy of Bookselling.

Many fewer potential publishers abroad have done a general arts degree before deciding what to do, as is common in Britain. Finally, and ironically, I should point out that, now the EC single market means that European national students do not have to pay fees at the universities of other member states, the largest overseas group at my old university is of German students. They are keen on the more paternalistic British system, which includes careers advice – rather than having to find everything out for themselves. Perhaps the wheel is turning full circle!

Conclusion

'So', said Dag Smith, when we met for lunch to discuss my findings in early 1993, 'are books different or aren't they?'

I started to hedge. Books fall into so many special categories, yet can be dismissed from each as not unique. For example, although the copyright of each published product belongs to someone, the moral rights of authorship are often hard to assert; newspapers have equal, if not more, power to influence the course of events; there are other trades that generate large numbers of new lines each year. But, at the same time, I doubt whether any other product beside the book crosses so many areas of difficulty concurrently.

The apocryphal story of a motorist stopping for directions and being told 'I wouldn't start from here' seems to apply with particular force to the publishing industry. There are so many factors, from the number of products to society's attitudes towards the book, that seem to cry out and make the case for special treatment. Publishing has a long way to travel before it is seen as the same as any other industry, and little collective will to get there anyway.

Yet at the same time, as I hope I have shown, marketing theory is now increasingly being applied to the selling of books, in all areas of the trade. For example, books today have far more of a high street presence; market research is being increasingly used by publishers and booksellers; print runs are getting longer; many firms are trying to produce fewer titles. And if you can implement the marketing theories that sell other sorts of product in the book trade, surely books are no different. Or are they?

In the spirit of realistic compromise, and bearing in mind the history of the industry, I must conclude that books still are slightly different, but are fast becoming less so.

Bibliography

Book Promotion, Sales and Distribution: A Management Training Course, Book House Training Centre/UNESCO 1991

Book Publishing in the United Kingdom, Key Facts 1981 – 88, The Publishers Association 1989

Dictionary of Marketing and Advertising, 2nd edition, Michael J Baker, Macmillan 1987

The Effective Use of Market Research, Robin J Birn, Kogan Page 1989

How to Market Books, Alison Baverstock, Kogan Page 1990

In Pursuit of Publishing, Alan Hill, John Murray in association with Heinemann Educational Books 1988

Inside Book Publishing: A Career Builder's Guide, Giles Clark, Blueprint 1988

Lost Book Survey: A Nationwide Survey of Book Buyers and Their Bookshop Purchases, Book Marketing Council and the Booksellers Association 1980

Marketing, 5th edition, Michael J Baker, Macmillan 1991

The Marketing Mirage: How to Make It a Reality, Colin McIver, Mandarin 1990

Marketing Strategy and Management, Michael J Baker, Macmillan 1985

Useful Addresses

The Association of Media Independents
34 Grand Avenue
London N10 3BP
081-883 9854

It put out the advertisements on why you should advertise through a recession.

Astron Appointments Ltd
20 – 24 Uxbridge Street
London W8 7TA
071-229 9171/6432
fax: 071-221 7594
Contacts: John Broom, Deborah Rea, Roger Stacey

Recruitment consultants – specialists in appointments throughout publishing.

Book Industry Communication (BIC)
39 – 41 North Road
London N7 9DP
071-607 0021
fax: 071-607 0415

Set up in April 1991 to oversee book trade standards, the organisation has six fronts on which it seeks progress: commercial message formats; bibliographic databases; machine readable codes; standard address numbers; sales and library management data; and distribution standards.

The Centre for the Book
The British Library
Great Russell Street
London WC1B 3DG
071-323 7608
fax: 071-323 7783
Executive Secretary: Mike Rump

DataMonitor
106 Baker Street
London W1M 1LA
071-625 8548
fax: 071-625 5080
Press Officer: Gina Allum

A strategic management consultancy that publishes over 150 market reports and industry surveys every year.

Euromonitor
87 – 88 Turnmill Street
London EC1M 5QU
071-251 8024
fax: 071-608 3149

Compilers of statistics and Book Report (a biennal survey).

Henley Centre for Forecasting Ltd
2 Tudor Street
London EC4Y 0AA
071-353 9961
fax: 071-353 2899
Contact: Bob Tyrrell

The Henley Centre examines the impact of economic and social change on business. Its goal is to provide clients with a detailed understanding of the factors affecting their markets, enabling them to plan for, and aspire to lead, change in the consumer environment. The Centre includes specialist econometric, macro-economic, international and UK social trends teams undertaking these types of analysis.

Independent Publishers Guild (IPG)
25 Cambridge Road
Hampton
Middlesex TW12 2JL
081-979 0250
Secretary: Yvonne Messenger

A support, information service and collective voice for independent publishers in Britain. Regular meetings and conferences, plus joint ventures to overseas events of interest (eg Frankfurt and Bologna Book Fairs). Most activities are London-based but there are several regional sub-groups. The Guild publishes a regular bulletin.

Publishers Publicity Circle
48 Crabtree Lane
London SW6 6LW
071-385 3708
Secretary: Christina Thomas

Monthly meeting place for book publicists from publishing houses and freelance PR agencies. Monthly newsletter, various awards and prizes.

The Society of Bookmen
c/o 12 Dyott Street
London WClA 2DF
071-836 8911
Secretary: Sally Whitaker

Market research

American Marketing Association
250 S Wacker Drive
Suite 200
Chicago
IL 6060-5819

Association of British Market Research Companies (ABMRC)
Secretary: Peter Jackling
c/o IDA Independent Analysts Ltd
22 – 23 Old Burlington Street
London W1X 1RL
071-439 3971
fax: 071-437 8867

Association of Market Survey Organisations (AMSO)
Secretary: Don Beverly
IRB International
Fenchurch House
101-111 High Road
London E18 2QP
071-505 9211
fax: 081-505 1333

Association of Users of Research Agencies (AURA)
Membership Secretary: Nick Stokes
c/o Boots the Chemist
Thane Road West
Nottingham NG2 3AA
0602 592063

Book Marketing Ltd
7a Bedford Square
London WC1B 3RA
071-580 7282
fax: 071-580 7236
Managing Director: Clare Harrison
Research Director: Leslie Henry

For more information see pages 111–116.

Chartered Institute of Marketing
Moor Hall
Cookham
Maidenhead
Berkshire SL6 9QH
0628 524922
fax: 0628 819195

European Market Research Association (ESOMAR)
J J Viottastraat 29
1071 JP
Amsterdam
Netherlands
31 20 664 2141
fax: 31 20 664 2922

Industrial Market Research Association (IMRA)
11 Bird Street
Lichfield
Staffordshire WS13 6PW
0543 263448
fax: 0543 250729

Market Research Society
15 Northburgh Street
London EC1V 0AH
071-490 4911
fax: 071-490 0608

The UK's professional association for those involved in compiling or using market social or economic research. All members must abide by a professional code of conduct.

Strategy, Research and Action Ltd
Marketing and Research Consultants
4th Floor
Parkway House
Sheen Lane
London SW14 8LS
081-878 9482
fax: 081-876 1204
Managing Director: Robin Birn

Founded in 1985, SR&A have specialised in serving smaller to medium-sized companies, and those businesses where management needs marketing education. Their client list now includes over 50 publishers in the UK, Europe and the USA.

The company also runs cooperative (and hence cost-effective) market research projects for publishers. The annual research study on maps, atlases and guides in the UK will be extended to the USA in 1993, and the company is setting up European research groups for dictionary specialists and map and guide publishers. SR&A have an associate company in the USA – Publishing Directions Inc.

Index